PUBLIC LIBRARY

W9-BOM-535

3 2500 503

DAVE
BARRY
TALKS
BACK

ALSO BY DAVE BARRY

The Taming of the Screw
Babies and Other Hazards of Sex
Stay Fit and Healthy Until You're Dead
Claw Your Way to the Top
Bad Habits
Dave Barry's Guide to Marriage and/or Sex
Homes and Other Black Holes
Dave Barry's Greatest Hits
Dave Barry Slept Here
Dave Barry Turns 40

DAVE BARRY TALKS BACK

BY DAVE BARRY

CARTOONS BY JEFF MacNELLY

Plainville Public Library
56 East Main Street
Plainville, Conn. 06062

CROWN PUBLISHERS, INC.   NEW YORK

Individual columns in this book first appeared in the *Miami Herald*
and are used with permission of the *Miami Herald*.
Copyright © 1991 by Dave Barry

All rights reserved. No part of this book may be reproduced or
transmitted in any form or by any means, electronic or mechanical,
including photocopying, recording, or by any information
storage and retrieval system, without permission in
writing from the publisher.

Published by Crown Publishers, Inc., 201 East 50th Street, New
York, New York, 10022. Member of the Crown Publishing Group.

CROWN is a trademark of Crown Publishers, Inc.

Manufactured in the United States of America

Book design by June Marie Bennett

Library of Congress Cataloging in Publication Data
Barry, Dave.
Dave Barry talks back/by Dave Barry—1st ed.
p. cm.
1. American wit and humor. 2. Newspapers—Sections,
columns, etc.—Humor. I. Title.
PN6162.B6296 1991
91-11139
814'.54—dc20
CIP

ISBN 0-517-58546-4

10 9 8 7 6 5 4 3 2 1

First Edition

818.5402

8/91

3 2535 04782 7503

*This book is dedicated to all the
Alert Readers who take the time to send
me newspaper items about exploding toilets
when they could be doing something
meaningful with their lives.*

ACKNOWLEDGMENTS

I thank the *Miami Herald* and all the other newspapers that run my column, except for the papers that cut out the booger jokes, which I bet they never do to George Will. I also thank my various editors, Tom Shroder, Gene Weingarten, David Groff, and Beth Barry, for telling me when things are NOT funny; and I thank Judi Smith and Doris Mansour for plausibly denying, when people call the office, that I even exist.

CONTENTS

Introduction   1

Introducing: Mr. Humor Person   6

(This Column Is Funny)   10

Blow-Up   16

Moby Yuck   21

The Bovine Comedy   25

Apocalypse Cow   29

Pop Goes the Weasel   34

Cheep Sex   39

Death by Toothpick   43

What Has Four Legs and Flies   47

Flying Fish   51

Amphibious Assault   56

Children May Be Hazardous to Your
Health   61

Attack of the Cartoon Animal Heads   66

Don't Box Me In   70

Un Nintended Benefits   74

Licking the Drug Problem   78

A Brush with Gardening   82

Captains Outrageous   86

Ship of Fools   90

Death Wormed Over   94

They Might Be Giants   98

Blimey! Frognal Cockfosters!   103

Dentists in Paradise   107

This Takes Guts   111

Taking the Zip Out of Zippy   116

Yellow Journalism   120

Just Say No to Rugs   125

Things That Go Hornk in the Night   129

Beetlejuice   134

Skivvying Up the Profits   138

Rotten to the Core   142

Well Endowed   146

Pranks for the Memories   150

Silent Night, Holy %*&?c   154

Garbage Scan   158

Where You Can Stick the Sticker Price   163

Lemon Harangue   167

Traffic Infraction, He Wrote   172

The Do-It-Yourself Deficit-Reduction
Contest   176

The Shocking Solution to the Budget
Deficit   181

Bug Off!   186

Insect Aside   190

Tax Fax   195

English, As It Were   200

It's a Mad, Mad, Mad, Mad World   205

Getting M*A*S*H*E*D   210

Taking the Manly Way Out   214

Life's a Hitch, and Then You Cry   218

Getting Physical 222

Stress for Success 226

Sports Nuts 230

The Male Animal 235

Male Fixations 239

The Web Badge of Courage 243

Confessions of a Weenie 248

Blood, Sweat, and Beers 252

An Offer They Can't Refuse 257

The Roll of the Humorist 262

Full-Bore Book Tour 266

Coffee? Tea? Weasel Spit? 270

I'm Dave. Fly Me. 274

We Will Barry You 279

Afterword 284

DAVE
BARRY
TALKS
BACK

INTRODUCTION

I am always getting letters from people who want my job.

"Dave," they start out. They always call me Dave.

"Dave," they say, "I want your job, because my current job requires me to be a responsible person doing productive work, whereas your job requires you mainly to think up booger jokes."

This kind of thoughtless remark really gets my dander up. Because although the reading public sees only the end product of my work, the truth is that I often spend many hours researching a particular topic before I make booger jokes about it. Take the Middle East. This is a very troubled region, a region fraught with complex and subtle issues of major international significance. You can't just sit down and dash off a column that says:

"The Middle East! Ha ha! What a bunch of boogerheads!"

No, there is a lot more to it than *that*. As a respected commentator, I am expected to produce a column that is thoughtful, insightful, profound, and—above all—

800 words long. Whereas the column above is only nine words, counting each "ha" as a separate word. So as a respected commentator I have to come up with another 791 words' worth of insights about the Middle East, such as: where it is,[1] and how come it is fraught with all these things, and what exactly we mean when we say our "dander" is up. According to the dictionary, "dander" means "temper," which would make sense except that I distinctly remember that a former editor of mine named Bob Shoemaker used to wear a little medallion around his neck that said:

I AM ALLERGIC TO HORSE DANDER.

Bob said he wore this so that in case he was ever rendered unconscious in an accident, the paramedics would realize that they should not expose him to horse dander. But if the dictionary is correct, Bob's medallion was actually saying that he should not be exposed to angry horses. You'd think the paramedics would already know this. You'd think that one of the first rules they learn in Paramedic School is, "Never expose an unconscious patient to an angry horse." Sheep, yes. We can all readily imagine situations where it would be necessary, even *desirable,* to expose an unconscious accident victim to an angry sheep. But as a respected commentator I am deeply concerned about this horse thing, which is just one more example of the kind of subtle and complex issue that we must come to grips with if we are ever to achieve any kind of meaningful understanding regarding these boogerheads in the Middle East.

---

[1] Not around here, I can tell you that.

2

Another question readers frequently ask is: "Dave, what specific system of writing do you use?"

Like many great writers such as Fyodor Dostoevsky and William Shakespeare, I use the Two-Dog System of writing. This system gets its name from the fact that it involves two dogs, one of which is your main dog and the other of which is your emergency backup dog, in case for any reason your main dog is unavailable. My main dog's name is Earnest, and my emergency backup dog is named Zippy. Every morning I get my coffee and say: "You want to go to WORK?" And the two of them charge for the door. Sometimes they charge right *into* the door, because they have the combined IQ of mayonnaise.

So the three of us go to my office, where we all take our positions:
- I sit in front of the computer and try to have insights;
- Earnest lies directly under my desk and periodically emits aromas;
- Zippy lies several feet away, ready to step in and emit aromas if Earnest experiences technical difficulties.

That, along with occasionally barking insanely at invisible beings, is the sum total of the dogs' contribution to the column effort. In the years we have worked together, neither dog, to the best of my recollection, has ever come up with a *single idea*. Sometimes I get just a little ticked off about this. "Hey Earnest!" I'll say. "How about you come up here and have insights while I go down there and emit aromas?" This causes Earnest to look at me and, drawing on the shrewd instincts that have made dogs so successful as a species despite having

3

no marketable skills, wag her tail. So the real burden of production rests entirely upon my shoulders, just as it rested upon the shoulders of Dostoevsky and Shakespeare, both of whom, you will notice, are currently dead.

My point is that, counting all the research, the fact-checking, the trips to the veterinarian, etc., there's a lot more to being a respected commentator than meets the eye. So as you read this book, I'll thank you not to pause every few sentences and remark: "Hey! *I* could write this crap!" Remember the wise words of the old Indian saying: "Before you criticize a man's collection of columns, walk a mile in his moccasins, bearing in mind that this is a good way to catch a fungus."

About Jeff MacNelly

I'm very pleased that Jeff MacNelly's illustrations will appear in this book, because he is, in my opinion, of all the illustrators in the world today, probably the tallest. Also he draws pretty well. He does some of his best work in bars. I've seen this a number of times. We'll go into a bar, and because Jeff is too modest to say anything, I'll take people quietly aside and say, "Do you know who that is? That's *Jeff MacNelly.*"

And the people, clearly impressed, will say, "Who?"

So I'll explain that Jeff has won about 17 Pulitzer Prizes and also draws the "Shoe" comic strip. This always gets a reaction. "Oh yeah!" they'll say. "Shoe! I love that one! Especially Opus the Penguin!"

Jeff is very gracious about this kind of adoration and will frequently take some place mats and do drawings for his fans, which is amazing to watch because *he never opens his eyes.* Really. I'm not even sure that he *has* eyes,

4

because nobody I know has ever seen them. He just sits there with his eyes closed, drawing things for people in the bar, and they get all excited and buy him beers. This makes me jealous because, as a writer, I can't do the same kind of thing. Usually I can't even bring my dogs *into* a bar. But at least my eyeballs are visible.

INTRODUCING:
MR. HUMOR PERSON

I frequently get letters from readers asking me to explain how humor works. Of course they don't ask in exactly those words. Their actual wording is more like: "Just where do you get off, Mr. Barry, comparing the entire legal profession to flatworms?" Or: "How about if I come down to that newspaper and stick a wastebasket up your nose?"

People come to me with this kind of probing question because I happen to be a major world expert on humor. I deal constantly with sophisticated humor questions such as: Would it be funnier to have the letter say, "How about if I come down to that newspaper and stick an IBM Selectric typewriter up your nose?" Or should I maybe try to work in a subtle political joke, such as: "How about if I come down to that newspaper and stick Vice President Quayle up your nose?" This is the kind of complex philosophical issue that I am forced to wrestle with, hour after hour, until 10:30 A.M., when "Wheel of Fortune" comes on.

After years of pursuing this regimen, I've learned

certain fundamental truths about humor. One of them is that "weasel" is a funny word. You can improve the humor value of almost any situation by injecting a weasel into it:

WRONG: "Scientists have discovered a 23rd moon orbiting Jupiter."

RIGHT: "Scientists have discovered a giant weasel orbiting Jupiter."

WRONG: "U.S. Rep. Newt Gingrich."

RIGHT: "U.S. Rep. Weasel Gingrich."

But the most important humor truth of all is that to really see the humor in a situation, you have to have perspective. "Perspective" is derived from two ancient Greek words: "persp," meaning "something bad that happens to somebody else," and "ective," meaning "ideally somebody like Donald Trump."

Take for example funerals. Funerals are not funny, which is why we don't laugh during them unless we just can't help ourselves. On the other hand, if a funeral occurs way on the other side of the world, and it involves the late Mr. Ayatollah "Mojo" Khomeini, and the mourners are so upset that they start grabbing garments and souvenir body parts off the deceased to the point where what's left of him could be laid to rest in a standard Good & Plenty box, then we have no choice but to laugh until our dentures fall into our laps.

An even better example of humor perspective involves a masseuse named Danette Sadle I met in San Francisco. (Let me stress, for the benefit of those readers who happen to be my wife, that I met her in a totally nonmassage situation.)

Danette had a regular client who decided to give her husband a professional massage as a gift, thinking that he would enjoy it. When the husband showed up, how-

Dave's HUMOR TIPS:

NOT FUNNY

Richard Nixon wearing a necktie.

FUNNY

Richard Nixon wearing a neck <u>weasel</u>.

ever, he was very nervous: He said he'd never had a massage before and he was concerned about getting undressed, and specifically whether he was supposed to leave his underpants on. Danette assured him that she was a professional and that he'd be covered at all times by a sheet, but he was still very concerned. So Danette said look, leave your underpants on, take them off, whatever makes you comfortable. Then she left the room while he undressed.

When she came back, the man was under the sheet looking as relaxed as a person being strapped down for brain surgery via ice pick. So Danette, trying to be as calm and nonthreatening as possible, walked up to him, reached out her hand, and touched the man's back at *exactly the moment* that the famous World Series earth-quake struck.

Let me stress that there was *nothing funny* about this earthquake, unless you have the perspective of hearing Danette describe how the man's entire body, in defiance of gravity, twitched violently into the air like a trout on amphetamines and landed on the other side of the room.

"It's usually more relaxing than this," said Danette.

"It's a good thing I kept my underpants on!" said the man.

These are words that a lot of people could stand to remember more often, but that is not my point. My point is that by having perspective on things we can find humor in virtually any situation, except of course for genuinely tragic events that cause serious trouble for large numbers of people. Or anything involving my car.

(THIS COLUMN
IS FUNNY)

Today we're going to attempt a ground-breaking medical experiment in an effort to help those unfortunate readers who suffer from a tragic condition called: Humor Impairment. Don't laugh! Humor Impairment afflicts Americans from all walks of life. Look at Richard Nixon. Here's a man whose sense of humor was so badly stunted that he was forced, at White House social functions, to wear special undershorts equipped with radio-controlled electrodes so that his aides could signal him, via electric shocks, when he was supposed to laugh. Sometimes, if the guests were unusually witty, the chief executive wound up twitching like a fresh-caught mackerel as dangerous voltage levels were reached in his boxers.

So it is possible for a Humor Impaired person, through courage and determination, to overcome his handicap, and maybe even someday, like Mr. Nixon, attain the ultimate political achievement of not getting indicted. But before we can treat Humor Impairment, we have to be able to recognize it. It can affect anyone.

Conquering Humor Impairment:

YOU could have it. To find out whether you do, ask yourself this: *What was your reaction to the first paragraph of this column?* Did you think: "Ha ha! That Nixon sure is a geek, all right!" Or did you think: "This is offensive, cheap, crude, and vicious humor, making fun of a former president of the United States, a major public figure, an internationally recognized elder statesman, just because he is a geek."

If you had either of those reactions, you are not Humor Impaired, because you at least grasped that the paragraph was *supposed* to be funny. The Humor Impaired people, on the other hand, missed that point entirely. They are already writing letters to the editor saying: "They wouldn't use electric shocks! They would use hand signals!" Or: "Where can I buy a pair of undershorts like that?" Trust me! I know these people! I hear from them all the time!

In fact, that's how I got the idea for the ground-breaking experiment. I had received a large batch of Humor Impaired letters responding to a column I wrote about Mister Language Person, and I was asking myself: How can I respond to these people in a humor column, when they don't understand that it's supposed to be humorous? That's when I came up with my ground-breaking idea. You know how some TV shows are "closed-captioned for the hearing impaired," meaning that if you have a special TV set, you can get subtitles? Well, I thought, why couldn't you do that with humor?

So the rest of this ground-breaking column will be *closed-captioned for the Humor Impaired.* After each attempted joke, the humor element will be explained in parentheses, so that you Humor Impaired individuals can laugh right along with the rest of us. Ready? Here we go:

Many readers were upset about a recent column by "Mister Language Person," the internationally recognized expert (NOT TRUE) who periodically answers common language questions submitted by imaginary readers (HE MAKES THE QUESTIONS UP). All of Mister Language Person's answers are intended to be as accurate (NOT TRUE) and informative (NOT TRUE) as is humanly possible while still containing words such as "booger." ("BOOGER" IS FUNNY.) No item is ever allowed to appear in Mister Language Person until trained grammarians have indicated their approval by barking at it in an excited manner. (THOSE ARE NOT GRAMMARIANS. THOSE ARE HIS DOGS.)

Although I had thought that the Mister Language Person column met the usual high standards of accuracy (EVERYTHING IN IT WAS WRONG), it contained an item that attracted a very large amount of mail from astute readers (SARCASM: THESE PEOPLE APPEAR TO BE MISSING KEY BRAIN LOBES) (NOT LITERALLY) who saw that, in one of the items, *something was wrong*. Yes! In a column that was basically a teeming, writhing mass of wrong answers, these keen observers were somehow able to detect: a wrong answer. (HEAVY SARCASM.)

The item that virtually all of these readers focused on was the one where an imaginary airline employee asked whether it was correct to say "A bomb has been placed on one of you're airplanes" or "A bomb has been placed, on one of you're airplanes," (THIS IS NOT REALLY HOW AIRLINES HANDLE BOMB THREATS) (AS FAR AS WE KNOW) and Mister Language Person replied that the correct wording was "A bomb has been placed IN one of you're airplanes." (GET IT? IT'S *STILL* WRONG!! HA HA!) Many readers felt this answer was incorrect and took time out from their busy and rewarding careers in the demanding field of food chewing (PROBABLY NOT TRUE) to write letters containing quotes such as—I am not making these up (HE IS NOT MAKING THESE UP)—"I was shocked with the grammar" and "Never have I seen such a mistake in grammer" and "I sure hope you remember this small bit of information, being as you are a writer you should have known it already."

Well, readers, I've researched this issue carefully

(NOT TRUE: HE DRANK A BEER), and although this is not easy for me to say, I have to admit it: Your right. Thanks for "straightening me out." This job would not be the same without you. I mean it. (HE MEANS IT.)

READER ALERT

EXPLODING THINGS

I don't wish to toot my own horn, but I definitely deserve to win several Nobel Prizes for the ground-breaking scientific work I've done in the field of exploding things. Since I wrote my first report, several years ago, about a snail that exploded in a restaurant in Syracuse, New York, I have received literally thousands of letters from alert readers sending me newspaper clippings about exploding ants, pigs, trees, yogurt containers, potatoes, television sets, finches, whales, municipal toilets, human stomachs, and of course cows. In accordance with standard journalism accuracy procedures, I never pass any of these reports on to the public without first reading it, saying to myself, quote, "Huh!" Using this process, I've determined that we have a worldwide exploding-thing epidemic on our hands, and until further notice we should all take the sensible precaution of avoiding things whenever possible. For example, you should never have bought this book.

BLOW-UP

Here at the Consumer Command Post ("Working To Make Your World More Threatening") we continue to receive alarming news items clipped out by alert readers who have somehow obtained scissors from their ward attendants. In accordance with our rigorous standards of accuracy, we have checked all of these submissions carefully to determine whether they contain any money, and now we are passing them along to you, the public, in hopes that you will be better able to make wise consumer choices and live a safer, healthier, and happier existence until such time as you burst into flames.

This is a very real possibility, according to a *Science Digest* article alertly mailed to us by Thomas Miller of Des Moines, Iowa ("More Than Just Pigs"). The article concerns spontaneous human combustion, which is when people, with no apparent cause, suddenly start burning like campfire marshmallows, reaching temperatures of thousands of degrees and being completely reduced to ashes. This is often fatal.

There are more than 200 reported cases of spontaneous human combustion, which can happen to anybody, anytime. "Persons have ignited while walking, driving, boating, and even dancing," notes *Science Digest*, reminding us of a number of evenings in the ninth grade when we, personally, came extremely close to erupting in flames right in the Harold C. Crittenden Junior High School cafeteria while dancing the Dirty Dig with Barbara Smayda to the song "Unchained Melody." Strangely, in many spontaneous human combustion cases, the area immediately around the victim is unaffected by the fire, although the ceiling and walls of the room are covered with oily soot.

No doubt you are asking yourself: "Is there anything that I, as an individual consumer, can do about this alarming problem?" Fortunately, there is. We've done some tests here at the Consumer Command Post, and we've found that you can get those walls looking "spick-and-span" again simply by scrubbing them with a mixture of detergent and warm water.

We feel we should warn you, however, that it is not a wise idea to put too many beauty products in your hair. We base this warning on a news article from *The State* of Columbia, South Carolina, sent in by Phyllis Wainscott, concerning a South Carolina woman who has filed a lawsuit claiming that her hair burst into flames because of the effect of the sun shining on two hair-care products that she was wearing. One of her attorneys is quoted—we are not making this up—as offering the following explanation:

"The whole thing is that she just put them on her head, both products, and—it was a hot day that day—and her head just spontaneously combusted."

Here's what gets our goat: Right now, the world scientific community is having multiple laboratory orgasms, just because some scientists *might* have discovered a "cold fusion" process whereby if you put atoms into a jar according to a certain recipe you *might* get a reaction that *might* someday be an important new energy source, but not until—trust us on this—the scientific community obtains a *large* amount of tax money donated by interested consumers. Meanwhile, here we have a South Carolina woman who, acting on her own, has apparently stumbled upon a proven energy-producing reaction requiring only a couple of readily available personal-grooming substances plus a human head! Think of the possibilities! We could see the day, in our

lifetimes, when a city the size of Baltimore, such as San Francisco, could have all of its electrical power needs met for a decade simply by harnessing the latent hairstyle energy of a single Republican Women's Club.

But we must not start rejoicing yet, not while we still face an ongoing epidemic of exploding items, a story we have been covering relentlessly for several months now in an unselfish effort to win a large cash journalism prize. So far we have reported the mysterious explosions of a snail, a cow, numerous pigs, and a human stomach, and we were asking ourselves: What next? And sure enough the answer was: municipal toilets. These were located in a courthouse in Seattle, where, according to news items sent in by approximately 40,000 alert readers, somebody connected an air compressor to the water line, so that when people attempted to flush, they were suddenly attacked by the Geyser From Hell. We can only hope that these people were not attorneys about to make important court appearances. ("Your Honor, may I approach the bench?" "No.")

And if you think that this is just an isolated incident, you are, no offense, an idiot. According to an Associated Press article alertly sent in by Lisa Hoffman, three people in Fordyce, Arkansas, were injured when somebody accidentally allowed propane to get into the city water supply, thus essentially transforming some toilets into bombs. Here is an actual quote from one of the victims: "Whomp, the commode burst into flames."

Well, consumers, we're out of space here, so unfortunately we can't report some of our other items, such as the one sent in by Charles Popelka concerning the woman in Ottumwa, Iowa ("It's Flat, But It's Quiet"), who encountered the exploding potato. But rest assured that, in the months ahead, we will continue to provide you consumers with information that will enable you to become sufficiently alarmed about the lethal threats that are all around us in everyday objects such as this keyboard that we are typing on, which we notice seems to be emitting some kind of WHOM

MOBY YUCK

Here at the Exploding Animal Research Institute we have received two very alarming news items that we are passing along today in the hopes that you, the generalized public, will finally break out of your apathetic, selfish, materialistic life-styles and send us some large cash contributions.

Item One, submitted by numerous alert readers, concerns the recent criminally insane vote by the U.S. Senate AGAINST having the federal government monitor methane emissions from cows. I am not making this vote up. As you may be aware, cows emit huge quantities of methane, which contributes to global warming, which has gotten so bad in some areas that brand-new shirts are coming out of the factory with armpit stains already in them. So the U.S. Senate (motto: "White Male Millionaires Working For You") was considering an amendment to the Clean Air Act, under which the government would monitor methane emissions from various sources, including "animal production."

Well, as you can imagine, this did not sit well with the

senators from those states where cow flatulence is a
cherished way of life. Leading the herd of opposition
senators was Senator Steve Symms of Idaho ("The Exploding Potato State"), who took the floor and stated
that the amendment would—this is an actual quote—
"put the nose of the federal government in almost every
place it does not belong."

So the Senate took out the part about monitoring
animal methane, which means there will be no advance
warning when, inevitably, there is some kind of cow-
interior blockage, causing a potentially lethal buildup of
flammable gasses and transforming one of these nor-
mally docile creatures into a giant mooing time bomb

which, if detonated, could cause the dreaded Rain of Organs. Have you ever, in a supermarket, accidentally encountered a cow tongue—a large sluglike slab of gray flesh that you couldn't imagine anybody purchasing for any purpose other than to nail it to the front door in hopes of scaring off evil spirits? Well, I'd like to know what Senator Symms would say if one of those babies came hurtling out of the sky and struck him at upwards of 100 miles per hour. "Yuck," would be my guess.

I base this statement on a similar situation in Oregon where innocent civilians were struck by falling whale parts. I am absolutely not making this incident up; in fact, I have it all on videotape, which I obtained from the alert father-son team of Dean and Kurt Smith. The tape is from a local TV news show in Oregon, which sent a reporter out to cover a 45-foot, eight-ton dead whale that washed up on the beach. The responsibility for getting rid of the carcass was placed upon the Oregon State Highway Division, apparently on the theory that highways and whales are very similar in the sense of being large objects.

So anyway, the highway engineers hit upon the plan—remember, I am not making this up—of blowing up the whale with dynamite. The thinking here was that the whale would be blown into small pieces, which would be eaten by sea gulls, and that would be that. A textbook whale removal.

So they moved the spectators back up the beach, put a half-ton of dynamite next to the whale, and set it off. I am probably guilty of understatement when I say that what follows, on the videotape, is the most wonderful event in the history of the universe. First you see the whale carcass disappear in a huge blast of smoke and flame. Then you hear the happy spectators shouting

"Yayy!" and "Wheee!" Then, suddenly, the crowd's tone changes. You hear a new sound, the sound of many objects hitting the ground with a noise that sounds like "splud." You hear a woman's voice shouting "Here comes pieces of . . . my GOD!" Something smears the camera lens.

Later, the reporter explains: "The humor of the entire situation suddenly gave way to a run for survival as huge chunks of whale blubber fell everywhere." One piece caved in the roof of a car parked more than a quarter of a mile away. Remaining on the beach were several rotting whale sectors the size of condominium units. There was no sign of the sea gulls, who had no doubt permanently relocated to Brazil.

This is a very sobering videotape. Here at the Institute we watch it often, especially at parties. But this is no time for gaiety. This is a time to get hold of the folks at the Oregon State Highway Division and ask them, when they get done cleaning up the beaches, to give us an estimate on the U.S. Capitol.

THE BOVINE
COMEDY

We do not wish to create a panic, but we are advising those of you who live in the Midwest to evacuate the area immediately and stay out until we can get to the bottom of this matter concerning the exploding cow.

We found out about this thanks to alert reader Dale Clemens, M.D., who sent us a very troubling article from the *Sun*. This is the same publication that broke the story three years ago about the rampage of the Giant Vampire Fleas, which were mutant fleas capable of sucking all the blood from small dogs within minutes and jumping 50 feet straight up, as the *Sun* put it, "without warning."

But as alarmed as we were by that article, we were even more alarmed by this new one, which is headlined: COW EXPLODES, HORRIFIED FARMER SUES. The story concerns a New Zealand farmer who purchased a cow, which he and his family were admiring, when suddenly —without warning, we bet—the cow "exploded before their eyes, spattering into a million bits of flesh and bone and drenching them all in blood."

Now, for most of us, when we hear of a shocking tragedy of this nature, our natural reaction is extreme sorrow that we were not able to observe it firsthand while wearing goggles. We estimate that, just from our immediate circle of friends, we could fill a municipal stadium with people willing to pay $50 apiece to see a cow spontaneously explode. But apparently this family prefers a cow that engages in more traditional cow behavior, such as a standing around exhibiting the intelligence of coleslaw, because the farmer is suing the breeder for selling him a "defective" cow. The article quotes a veterinarian as saying that cows produce up to three quarts of gas per minute. "If it can't burp," the veterinarian says, "its stomach can explode within the hour."

This is exactly the kind of story the Founding Fathers had in mind when they put the clause in the Constitution stating that the press has the right to run up enormous long-distance telephone charges. So we called up New Zealand, which is in the Mars Time Zone, but we were unable to locate any of the people named in the exploding cow story. We were actually starting to wonder if the *Sun* story was untrue when suddenly, without warning, an alert reader named Donald McEwan sent us *another* frightening cow-related news item. This one came from the *Washington Post,* and it stated—we are not making any of this up—that a Colorado State University animal-nutrition professor named Donald Johnson has been studying cow flatulence for 20 years, and has determined that the average cow emits 200 to 400 quarts of methane *per day,* resulting in a total annual world cow methane output of 50 million metric *tons.*

(Campers: This is yet another argument for NEVER allowing a cow inside your sleeping bag.)

So, of course, we called Professor Johnson, who

seemed remarkably normal considering his chosen field, and we asked him whether cows can explode.

"I've never heard of it," he said. "It's rather unlikely that a cow would actually explode, although there is considerable methane gas and in some cases it could be present in concentrations that could ignite."

In fact, Professor Johnson revealed that on more than one occasion, in college classrooms, he has used a candle to set fire to emissions being emitted by live cows, one of whom was able to sustain the flame *without the candle.*

Ask yourself this question: What if such a cow were to fall into the wrong hands? Picture this: You're on a seemingly routine commercial airline flight, rummaging around your breakfast tray in search of an implement sharp enough to penetrate your "omelet," when suddenly, without warning, from back in the smoking section, you hear sharp cries of:

"Look out!"

And:

"He's got a cow!"

You whirl around, and there, in the aisle, stands: a terrorist. In one hand he holds a Bic lighter; in the other he holds a fuse, which is attached to Professor Johnson's high-output cow—which by the way would not be detected by any airport metal detector currently in use—and in the next instant the entire cabin is filled with the chilling, unmistakable sound of: The Death Moo.

What can we do to prevent this chilling scenario from becoming a reality or—even worse—a made-for-television "docu-drama"? Clearly what is called for is a federal task force, ideally headed by Dan Quayle, who seems to have a lot of spare time, assuming that he is not called upon to suddenly, without warning, become president of the United States. We urge you to write a letter about this to your congressperson, bearing in mind that if he is an average adult, he produces, according to the *Washington Post*, about one liter of methane per day.

APOCALYPSE COW

I have wonderful news for those of you who were disappointed when the world failed to end last year.

In case you missed it, what happened last year was that a man named Edgar Whisenant, who is a former NASA rocket engineer, came out with a booklet in which he proved via exact mathematical calculations based on the Bible that the world was going to end in 1988, most likely on September 12. I first heard Mr. Whisenant explain this on a radio show one morning when I was in New Orleans for the Republican convention. At the time I was thrilled, because I had spent the previous evening with some other trained journalists at an establishment named Nick C. Castrogiovanni's Original Big Train Bar, which features a specialty drink that comes in a large foam container shaped like a toilet, and as far as I was concerned the world could not end soon enough. A lot of other True Believers around the country also got very excited over Mr. Whisenant's prediction, so you an imagine what a letdown it was when

September 12 rolled around and—as you know if you keep up with the news—the world did not end, which meant among other things that we had to go ahead with this presidential election.

Well, guess what. Mr. Whisenant has just come out with another booklet, and in Chapter 1 (entitled "What Went Wrong in 1988") he graciously admits that there was an error in his calculations. He now scientifically calculates that the world will probably end on—mark it in your appointment calendar—this coming September 1. Yes! *Before the World Series.*

So you need to get ready. You need to prepare for The End by doing some real "soul searching" and ask-

ing yourself this hard question: "If the world ended tomorrow, could I honestly say that I have done everything I could, as a spiritual person, to run up my VISA balance?" Think about it! Because come September 1 it's all over. All the people who have led moral lives will go straight to heaven, whereas you and your friends are going to suffer through seven years of wars, plagues, famines, and sitting in a small room while a man named "Nate" explains the advantages of time-sharing. And then you will go to hell, which as you frequent fliers know is located in Concourse D of O'Hare International Airport. See you there!

Please bear in mind, however, that just because the world is coming to an end does NOT mean that you are relieved of your civic responsibility to be alarmed about the ongoing international epidemic of exploding organisms. I regret to report that the situation has worsened drastically, to the point where we here at the National Exploding Organism Alarm Bureau (B.O.O.M.) are declaring a Condition Red Alert Mode Status Condition.

As you know if you read this column regularly but have retained some brain functionality, over the past year we have gone through an escalating series of Alert Conditions in response to documented reports of organisms exploding, as follows:

1. **CONDITION YELLOW:** Snail.
2. **CONDITION BROWN:** Pig, Cow.
3. **CONDITION YUCK-O-RAMA:** Human stomach, municipal toilets.
4. **CONDITION POTATO:** Potato.

But we are now forced to declare Condition Red in response to a recent deluge of letters from readers who want to know the proper pronunciation of "deluge."

Also we have received many alarming new reports of exploding organisms. For example, each of the following items was submitted by several Alert Readers:

- The *Chicago Tribune* reported that a bison at the Atlanta Zoo "was overfed and then transported in a truck. Its stomach exploded en route, killing the animal."

- The *Baltimore Sun* reported that when a 40-ton whale carcass turned up in Baltimore harbor, sightseers were kept away because, according to a federal official, the decomposing whale "might explode."

- The *National Law Journal* reported that a man is suing the Arm & Hammer baking soda company, claiming that after he took some baking soda for indigestion, his bison exploded. No! Wait! He claims his *stomach* exploded. Sorry if we alarmed you.

- The *Virginian-Review* in Covington, Virginia, published a column entitled "Aunt Mary's Letter Box," at the top of which is a drawing of a sweet-looking elderly lady with wire-rimmed glasses. The first letter asks how to get rid of pesky black ants. Here's Aunt Mary's answer, which I swear I am not making up: "Make a small ring of jelly and in the center place some yeast. The ants will eat through the jelly and then get to the yeast. After they eat the yeast they will explode." Ha ha! That Aunt Mary! I'd love to find out how she got rid of pesky Uncle Bill.

But this is no time for speculation. No, this is a time for courage. There's an inspirational saying that high-school football coaches use to send their young "gladiators" out onto the "battlefield" to have their knee cartilage turned into "gumbo," and it goes like this: "When the going gets tough, everybody should crawl under the dinette table of his or her choice and commence whimpering." If you have no dinette table, you should purchase one, scheduling your payments to start sometime after September 1.

POP GOES
THE WEASEL

This is getting scary.

I am referring to the alarming increase in the number of spontaneously exploding animals. If you read this column regularly, you definitely need to get some kind of therapy, but you also are aware that we have repeatedly presented documentary proof of explosions involving the following broad spectrum of animal life:

1. A snail.
2. A cow.

The snail, you will recall, exploded in a restaurant in Syracuse, New York, whereas the exploding cow was in New Zealand. So clearly we are looking at a Global Trend, yet our so-called "leadership" remains silent. What is it going to take? Must we wait until the president of the United States, demonstrating his concern for Agriculture, poses for a photo opportunity at a dairy farm, and suddenly the air is filled with the unmistakable sound ("whumph") of detonating beef, and the leader of the Free World is caught in a hail of bovine

The Exploding PiG: Alarming new Airport Security Implications.

GATES →

DEATH TO (YOUR NAME HERE)

organs, including up to four stomachs, traveling at up to 350 miles per hour? Wouldn't that be *great*? Ha ha!

Fine, go ahead and have your cheap sophomoric laughs. But perhaps you will not be so amused when we report the shocking information we have obtained recently concerning:

EXPLODING PIGS

Yes. *Pigs.* This was brought to our attention by several alert readers who sent us an article from the *Weekly World News,* a respected supermarket-checkout publication whose journalism motto is *"Licentia Vatun Veritatis"* (literally, "Leech Boy Eats Mom"). The article concerns farmers in Brazil who are upset because their pigs, as the *News* sensitively puts it, "are exploding like bombs." In case anyone might have the slightest doubt about the accuracy of this story, there is an actual photograph of a pig, which has been cut in half (we're talking about the photograph), with the word "BANG!" realistically inserted between the two halves. Case closed!

So we now have solid evidence of explosions in *three* species of animals. And that, we fear, is not all. This whole animal situation is turning out to be a lot like an iceberg, where you see only a small portion sticking up in the air, but when you look below the surface, you discover a huge quantity of exploding penguins. Because lately we have been receiving a *lot* of alarming animal-related news articles, such as the one concerning the:

VIOLENT SPORTSWEAR-OBSESSED ATTACK OWL

Alert reader Joyce Schwettman sent in this article, from the *Anchorage Daily News,* concerning a man named Bruce Talbot who was skiing in a park, minding his own business, when a great horned owl swooped down and, over the course of the next few minutes, relieved the increasingly alarmed Mr. Talbot of the following articles of clothing: his hat, his gloves, his coat, his vest, and finally his *shirt*. We are not making this up. The owl would get his talons into a garment, and the only way Mr. Talbot could escape was to remove the garment, and then the owl would latch on to *another* garment, and so on until the owl had assembled almost a complete ski-wear ensemble and Mr. Talbot was half-naked and skiing for his life, hoping to make it to safety before the owl developed a hankering for his pants.

The article quotes a wildlife official as saying that great horned owls "regularly" attack people. "They have very powerful feet," the official says, leading us to believe that it is just a matter of time before these creatures are employed by automobile dealerships ("No thanks really, I was just look . . . HEY! Let GO!!").

But we don't want to think about that now. Right now we want to devote all our mental energy to trying to comprehend an article from the Montgomery County, Maryland, *Journal,* alertly sent to us by C. H. Breedlove, Jr., concerning a:

DRAMATIC LOBSTER RESCUE

You're going to be *sure* that we made this up, but we didn't. It seems that a Rockville, Maryland, restaurant called The House of Chinese Gourmet installed a lobster tank, which greatly upset some customers who belong to a group called the People for the Ethical Treatment of Animals, whose members apparently have (1) a deep respect for all living things and (2) a tremendous amount of spare time. They bought seven lobsters from the restaurant for $40, removed them from the tank (according to the article, a PETA member "talked softly and rubbed the lobsters to reassure them"), and then paid $200 to fly the lobsters to Portland, Maine, where they (the lobsters) were released in the ocean, where we are sure they will live happy, productive lives until they are recaptured by lobstermen, who will re-sell them to The House of Chinese Gourmet, which will re-sell them to PETA, and thus will the Great Cycle of Life continue until the lobsters become so airsick that they deliberately hurl themselves into boiling water.

Our final alarming item is an Associated Press photograph, sent in by various readers, showing an Afghan Freedom Fighter using a rocket-propelled grenade launcher—no doubt paid for with our tax dollars—to shoot at *fish*. We thought you PETA members should know.

CHEEP SEX

Many, many of you have written to me asking the following question: "Dave, are there any new developments in the field of artificial falcon insemination, and could these developments help improve the American electoral process?"

I am pleased to report that the answer to both questions is "yes." I have received some very exciting information on this subject from alert reader Lance Waller, who sent me an article from the April issue of *Smithsonian* magazine concerning the World Center for Birds of Prey in Boise, Idaho. The Center is engaged in the preservation of falcons, fierce birds of prey that are named after the Ford Falcon, which holds the proud title of Slowest Car Ever Built. In certain areas of the country you can go to a stoplight and find Falcon drivers who pressed down on their accelerators in 1963 and are *still waiting* for their cars to move.

Anyway, the scientists at the Center are trying to breed falcons, sometimes via artificial insemination, which means they (the scientists) have to get hold of some falcon semen, which you cannot simply pick up in your local supermarket. (Well, OK, you CAN, but it's not fresh.)

So according to *Smithsonian* magazine, these scientists obtain the semen via a process so wondrous that you will insist I made it up, but I did not. Here, according to the article, is how it works: First, a falcon handler hand-feeds a baby male falcon, which eventually "regards its handler as another falcon." Then, when the falcon matures, the handler goes into a chamber with it and they engage in a courtship ritual, wherein they bow their heads and make cheeping sounds. "The two of them

provide an amazing spectacle," states the article, "man and bird bowing and cheeping, affectionate lovers arousing each other."

Then the handler puts on—remember, I am not making this up—"a nondescript fedora with a rubber dam around the crown to catch the semen." He turns around, and the falcon "flies to the hat and, with much cheeping and fluttering of wings, copulates with it."

The magazine has an actual photograph of this, showing a man with his arms folded, wearing a facial expression that would look somber and dignified, suitable for a portrait painting of a bank president, except that the man is wearing an extremely comical hat, on top of which is this large, wildly excited bird experiencing a Climactic Moment. (The article doesn't say what happens next, but I like to think they smoke tiny cigarettes.)

Anyway, looking at this picture, I couldn't help but think about the American electoral process. You know how your top political figures traditionally demonstrate their qualifications for high government office by putting on virtually any form of cretin headwear that is handed to them? Well, think how it would be if, during the 1992 presidential campaign, some leading presidential contender was making an appearance in Iowa, and some innocent-looking Girl Scout handed him what she claimed was a special ceremonial headdress, and he put it on, and his head suddenly became a highly erotic stimulant for major birds of prey ("In a surprise campaign development that raises delicate legal issues, Rep. Dick Gephardt was carried off today by a large, cheeping flock of lust-crazed, federally protected falcons").

Wouldn't that be wonderful? Wouldn't that transform the presidential campaign from an endless droning bore into something you'd genuinely look forward to on the TV news? Oh, I know what you're thinking. You're thinking, "But what if the politicians *like* it? What if they start wearing their hats *all the time?* What if, say, the vice president starts wearing one to formal foreign funerals? Where would he get a hat small enough? Certainly these are large hurdles, but I am certain that, as a nation, we will find a way to overcome them. But not right now. Right now I have to go. Rex is chirping for me.

DEATH BY TOOTHPICK

Here at the Bureau of Medical Alarm, we continue to receive shocking new evidence that being human is an extremely dangerous occupation that probably should be prohibited by law.

For example, consider the alarming article sent in by alert reader Jessica Bernstein from the August 10, 1984 issue of the *Journal of the American Medical Association*, entitled "Toothpick-Related Injuries in the United States, 1979 Through 1982." This article notes with concern that although toothpicks "are long, slender, hard, sharp, and indigestible, they are rarely considered objects of potential injury and death." Yes! Death! The article reports that during the period studied, there have been thousands of toothpick-related injuries and three actual fatalities.

What gets our goat, here at the Bureau of Medical Alarm, is that these needless tragedies could be avoided if the government would simply require all toothpicks to carry this printed message:

WARNING: THE SURGEON GENERAL HAS DE-

TERMINED THAT YOU SHOULD NOT SWALLOW THIS TOOTHPICK OR STAB YOURSELF IN THE EYEBALL WITH IT WHILE TRYING TO READ THIS WARNING.

Why hasn't this been done? When will the politicians stop knuckling under the powerful toothpick lobby, with its easy money, fast boats, and loose women? How come powerful lobbies never send loose women down here to the Bureau of Medical Alarm? These are some of the questions that were very much on our minds until we were distracted by an even more alarming article, sent in by alert reader Betsy Powers, from the July 5, 1980 issue of the *British Medical Journal.* Unfortunately we cannot be too specific about this article, because this is a family newspaper (it has a wife newspaper and two little baby newspapers at home). All we can say is that the article involves an upsetting development that can occur when a well-known male bodily part gets too close to a working vacuum cleaner. This seems to be a fairly common occurrence, at least in Britain. The article contains the following quotations, which we swear we are not making up, although for reasons of tastefulness, the bodily part will be referred to as "Morton" (not its real name):

"Case 1—A 60-year-old man said that he was changing the plug of his Hoover Dustette vacuum cleaner in the nude while his wife was out shopping. It 'turned itself on' and caught his Morton. . . ."

"Case 2—A 65-year-old railway signalman was in his signal box when he bent down to pick up his tools and caught his Morton in a Hoover Dustette, 'which happened to be switched on.' "

These quotations definitely touched a nerve here at the Bureau of Medical Alarm. Clearly males need to be more careful, especially if they get naked anywhere near a Hoover Dustette, which is apparently auditioning for a role as a major appliance in *Fatal Attraction II*.

What you are no doubt saying to yourself now is, "Hmmmm, I wonder if there have been any similar incidents involving lobsters." We regret to report that the answer is yes, as we learned from an article alertly sent in by Janice Hill (notice that it is women who are sending these articles in).

This article concerns a man who attempted to steal a lobster from a Boston fish market by stuffing it (the lobster) down the front of his pants. The lobster had been wearing those rubber-band handcuffs, but appar-

ently they slipped off, and the lobster, with revenge on its tiny mind, angrily grasped hold of the first thing it found, and we will not go into what happened next, except to say that, if you are a guy, it makes a toothpick to the eyeball sound like a day at the Magic Kingdom.

We actually have MORE alarming medical items here, including a really good one about a moth that flew into a noted Denver attorney's ear canal and refused to come out voluntarily. But we're running out of space, so we'll just close with this Health Reminder: Don't smoke or drink. Or eat. Or go outside. Or breathe. And men: If you MUST change a major-appliance plug in the nude, PLEASE wear a condom.

WHAT HAS FOUR LEGS
AND FLIES

People often say to me, "Dave, when you say you're not making something up, does that mean you're really and truly not making it up?" And the answer is yes. Meaning no, I am not making it up. I mention this so you'll believe me when I say that I'm not making up today's topic, which is: the Head-Smashed-In Buffalo Jump.

The Head-Smashed-In Buffalo Jump is a historical site and tourist attraction in Alberta, Canada. Canada, as you know, is a major important nation boasting a sophisticated, cosmopolitan culture that was tragically destroyed last week by beavers.

Ha ha! Don't mind me. I like to toss out little "zingers" about Canada from time to time because I enjoy getting mounds of letters from irate Canadians who are Sick and Tired of Americans belittling Canada and who often include brochures full of impressive Canadian Facts such as that Canada is the world's largest producer of magnesium dentures as well as the original home of Michael J. Fox, Big Bird, Plato, etc.

The thing is, I like Canada. It's clean, and it makes

good beer. Also it has a spirit of general social cooperation that you find lacking in the States, a good example being the metric system. You may recall that a while back we were all supposed to convert to the metric system from our current system of measurement, which is technically known as the "correct" or "real" system. The metric conversion was supposed to result in major economic benefits deriving from the fact that you, the consumer, would suddenly have no idea how the hell much anything cost. Take coleslaw. Under the current system, coleslaw is sold in easily understood units of measurement called "containers," as in "Gimme one of them containers of coleslaw if it's fresh." In a metric supermarket, however, the deli person would say, "How much do you want? A kilometer? A hectare? Hurry up! My break starts in five liters!" You'd get all confused and wind up buying enough coleslaw to fill a wading pool, and the economy would prosper.

So the metric conversion was clearly a good idea, and when the government started putting up metric highway signs (SPEED LIMIT 173 CENTIPEDES) Americans warmly responded by shooting them down. Thus the metric system did not really catch on in the States, unless you count the increasing popularity of the nine-millimeter bullet.

Meanwhile, the Canadians, being cooperative, quietly went ahead and actually converted. I know this because I was on a Canadian radio program once, and the host announced that the temperature was "8." This was obviously a lie, so I asked him about it, and he confided, off the air, that the real temperature, as far as he knew, was around 40. But then his engineer said he thought it was more like 50, and soon other radio personnel were chiming in with various other interpretations of "8,"

and I was struck by the fact that these people had cheerfully accepted, in the spirit of cooperation, a system wherein *nobody really knew what the temperature was.* (The correct mathematical answer is: chilly.)

The point I am making is that Canada is a fascinating and mysterious country, which is why we should not be surprised to learn that it is the location of the Head-Smashed-In Buffalo Jump historical site and tourist attraction. I found out about this from an extremely alert reader named Sandy LaFave, who sent me an article from the *Fort McLeod Tourist Greeter* that explains the whole buffalo-jump concept.

It seems that many moons ago (in metric, 14.6 mega-moons) North America was occupied by large and fortunately very stupid herds of buffalo. Certain Native American tribes used to obtain their food by disguising themselves in buffalo skins and going from tepee to tepee shouting "Trick or Treat!"

No, seriously, according to the *Fort McLeod Tourist Greeter,* they disguised themselves so they could lure a buffalo herd closer and closer to a cliff, then stampede it over the edge. That's where the "Buffalo Jump" part of the name comes from. The "Head-Smashed-In" part comes from a native legend, which holds that one time a young brave (probable tribal name: "Not Nuclear Physicist") decided to watch the hunt while standing *under* the cliff. According to the *Tourist Greeter,* he "watched the buffalo topple in front of him like a mighty waterfall. . . . When it was over and the natives were butchering the animals, they found him under the pile of dead buffalo with his head smashed in."

Even thousands of years later, it is difficult to ponder this tragedy without choking back large, moist snorts of anguish. But some good has come of it. The Head-Smashed-In Buffalo Jump has been declared a World Heritage Site ("as are the pyramids in Egypt and the Taj Mahal in India," notes the *Tourist Greeter*). The Alberta government has constructed an interpretive centre (note metric spelling) where activities are held. "There's always something to see and do at the Head-Smashed-In Buffalo Jump Interpretive Centre and this summer is no exception," states an official schedule. I have called the centre, and when they answer the phone, they say, very politely—I absolutely swear this is true—"Head-Smashed-In, may I help you?"

And the scary part is, I think maybe they *can.*

FLYING FISH

We certainly do not wish to cause widespread panic, but we are hereby warning the public to be on the lookout for falling trout.

We base this warning on an alarming article from the *Bangor Daily News,* sent in by alert reader Jane Heart, headlined TORPEDO APPROACH USED TO STOCK LAKES WITH TROUT. According to the article, the Maine Department of Inland Fisheries is restocking lakes by dropping trout from airplanes. A hatchery official notes that the trout, which weigh about a pound each, drop from 100 to 150 feet "like hundreds of little torpedoes."

This article should cause extreme concern on the part of anyone who is familiar with gravity, which was discovered in 1684 by Sir Isaac Newton, who was sitting under a tree when an apple landed on his head, killing him instantly. A one-pound trout would be even worse. According to our calculations, if you dropped the trout from 150 feet, it would reach a speed of . . . let's see, 150 feet times 32 feet per second, at two pints to the liter, minus the radius of the hypotenuse, comes to . . .

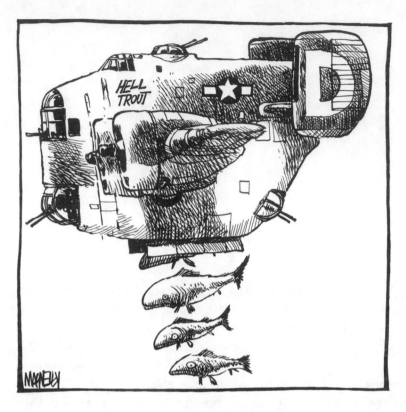

a high rate of speed. Anybody who has ever seen a photograph showing the kind of damage that a trout traveling that fast can inflict on the human skull knows that such photographs are very valuable. I paid $20 for mine.

And yet here we see Maine, which we usually think of as a quiet, responsible state known primarily for sleet, deliberately causing potentially lethal fish to hurtle at high velocities toward Earth, residence of many members of the public.

Oh, I realize the program is not *designed* to harm the public. But even highly trained pilots are not perfect. Consider the three pilots who were recently convicted of flying drunk on a commercial flight, during which they aroused suspicion by instructing the passengers to fasten their seat belts because of "snakes in the engine." I am not accusing the Maine Department of Inland Fisheries of using drunk pilots, but if one of them *did* have a few, and happened to fly over, say, a Shriners convention while carrying a full load of trout, the temptation to let those babies go would be irresistible. To us, anyway.

What is especially alarming is that this is not the first time that government agencies have dropped potentially lethal creatures from planes. An even scarier example is discussed in an article in the October 1990 issue of *Air Force* magazine, which was alertly sent to us by John Breen. The article, by C. V. Glines, is entitled "The Bat Bombers," and we urge you to read the whole thing yourself, because otherwise you are not going to believe us.

In brief, here's what the article says:

In December 1941, shortly after Pearl Harbor, a Pennsylvania dental surgeon named Lytle S. Adams thought of a way that the United States could fight back against Japan. It will come as no surprise to anyone who has undergone dental surgery that the idea he came up with was: attaching incendiary bombs to bats and dropping them out of airplanes. The idea was that the bats would fly into enemy buildings, and the bombs would go off and start fires, and Japan would surrender.

So Dr. Adams sent his idea to the White House, which laughed so hard that it got a stomachache.

No! That's what you'd *expect* to happen, but instead the White House sent the idea to the U.S. Army, which, being the U.S. Army, launched a nationwide research effort to determine the best kind of bat to attach a bomb to. By 1943 the research team had decided on the free-tailed bat, which "could fly fairly well with a one-ounce bomb." Thousands of these bats were collected and—remember, we are not making any of this up—placed in ice-cube trays, which were then refrigerated to force the bats to hibernate so bombs could be attached to them. On May 23, 1943, a day that every schoolchild should be forced to memorize, five groups of test bats, equipped with dummy bombs, were dropped from a B-25 bomber flying at 5,000 feet. Here, in the dramatic words of the article, is what happened next:

"Most of the bats, not fully recovered from hibernation, did not fly and died on impact."

Researchers continued to have problems with bats failing to show the "can-do" attitude you want in your night-flying combat mammal. Also there was an incident wherein "some bats escaped with live incendiaries aboard and set fire to a hangar and a general's car."

At this point the Army, possibly sensing that the project was a disaster, turned it over to the Navy. Really. "In October 1943, the Navy leased four caves in Texas and assigned Marines to guard them," states the article. The last thing you want, in wartime, is for enemy agents to get hold of your bats.

The bat project was finally canceled in 1944, having cost around $2 million, which is a bargain when you consider what we pay for entertainment today.

But our point is, the government has a track record of dropping animals out of airplanes, and there is no reason to believe that this has stopped. Once the government gets hold of a truly bad idea, it tends to cling to it. For all we know, the Defense Department is testing bigger animals, capable of carrying heavier payloads. We could have a situation where, because of an unexpected wind shift, thousands of semi-frozen, parachute-wearing musk oxen come drifting down into a major population center and start lumbering confusedly around with high explosives on their backs. We definitely should have some kind of contingency plan for stopping them. Our best weapon is probably trout.

AMPHIBIOUS ASSAULT

You can imagine how alarmed I was when I found out that I had been swimming in the same waters as the Giant Perverted Turtle. Unless of course you have not yet heard about the Giant Perverted Turtle, in which case please be advised that, until we get this thing cleared up, you should avoid submerging yourself in any body of water unless it has a drain and a soap dish.

I found out about this story when numerous alert readers sent me an article from the *Reporter,* a newspaper published in the Florida Keys, headlined TURTLE ATTACK IS REPORTED. Immediately I interrupted my regular journalism routine of staring fixedly at individual pieces of ceiling dirt, because it just so happens that my major hobby, aside from turning off lights and appliances that have been turned on days earlier by my son, is scuba diving off the Florida Keys. You go out to the reef, bouncing over the waves, then you dive in and admire the incredible variety of marine life that is attracted by other diving enthusiasts barfing over the side of the charter boat.

No, really, you see some fascinating things down there. I once got to see what fishing looks like from the fish end. There, dangling in the current, was a largish hook, to which had been attached a disgusting thing such as you might be served in a sushi restaurant. Staring at this thing was a small formal gathering of filefish, which is a fish with pursed lips and a bulging forehead that make it look very serious, as though it should be carrying a little briefcase and doing the other fishes' tax returns. As the other filefish watched, the first one would swim forward, take the sushi in its mouth, spit it out immediately, then swim to the end of the line. Then the next fish would repeat this procedure, and the next, and so on ("Yuck! You try it, Norm!" "OK! Yuck! You try it, Walter!" "OK! Yuck! You try . . ."). If I'd had a waterproof pen and paper with me, I'd have stuck a little note on the hook saying, "THEY DON'T LIKE IT."

This experience gave me an idea. Remember when President Bush was taking his biweekly vacation up in Kenneth E. Bunkport IV, Maine, and he failed to catch any fish, day after day, until it became a national news story of greater urgency than Lebanon, and the whole federal government apparatus seemed to shudder to a halt while the Leader of the Free World, the man most responsible for dealing with pressing and increasingly complex national and international issues, was off somewhere trying to outwit an organism with a brain the size of a hydrogen atom? Well my idea is, next time we have this problem, we send some U.S. Naval frogpersons down there to attach a fish manually to the presidential hook. These would have to be trusted frogpersons, not pranksters, because America would definitely be a laughingstock among nations if the president were to engage in a fierce three-hour angling struggle and finally, triumphantly, haul out, say, a sheep.

But before we implement this program, we need to do something about the Giant Perverted Turtle. According to the *Reporter* article, written by outdoor writer Bob T. Epstein, there's a very aggressive male 300-pound loggerhead turtle that lurks in the water under one of the bridges in the Florida Keys and—I am not making this up—keeps trying, very forcefully, to *mate with human divers*. What is worse, Epstein says, in at least one case the turtle actually *succeeded*. I'm not going to give details of this occurrence in a family newspaper, except to say that if we ever decide we need some form of punishment harsher than the death penalty, this would be a strong candidate.

JUDGE: I sentence the defendant to be put in the lagoon with Bart.

DEFENDANT: NO! NOT THE TURTLE!

I called up one of the divers who'd reportedly been attacked, a real estate agent named Bruce Gernon, who confirmed the whole thing, but asked me to stress that he successfully fought the turtle off. So let the record show that the turtle did not get to first base with Mr. Gernon. But clearly we have a serious problem here. Bob Epstein told me that, since his story appeared, he has been contacted almost daily by people who have been molested by large sea creatures but never told anybody. "This is a sensitive area," Epstein said. "People are reluctant to talk about that aspect of their relationships with turtles or seals or dolphins or walruses."

Did you hear that? *Walruses.*

(DEFENDANT: NOOOOO!!)

Fortunately this alarming story is getting attention

from leading science authorities: Epstein told me he had been contacted by both the Letterman and Sajak shows. So action is being taken, and not a moment too soon, either, because—this appears to be a related story —several alert readers have sent me an Associated Press article stating that two marine biologists in a submarine 690 feet deep, far off the coast of Alaska, discovered, lying on the ocean floor: a cow. I am still not making this up. Needless to say the cow was deceased. God alone knows how it got there. One obvious possibility is prankster frogpersons, but we cannot rule out the pos-

sibility that the cow was abducted by lust-crazed wal-ruses. Fortunately the biologists were able to make a videotape, starring Rob Lowe, so we should have some answers soon. Until then, I'm not going to even take a shower. Not that this is anything *new*.

CHILDREN
MAY BE HAZARDOUS
TO YOUR HEALTH

It's time for Alarming Medical News Items, the popular feature that can strike at any time without warning symptoms. For your protection, this column undergoes a rigorous fact-checking procedure under which, before we will print an item, it must first be delivered to us by the United States Postal Service. Don't bother to thank us: We aren't listening.

Speaking of which, our first alarming item concerns the recently discovered:

EAR PROBLEM FROM HELL

We learned about this thanks to alert reader Diane Eicher, who sent in an American Medical Association newsletter containing an article about a North Carolina man who went to his doctor complaining of a "full sensation" in one ear, accompanied by a hearing loss. The doctor checked it out, and found that the man's ear canal was blocked by—we are not making this up—a plug of hardened Super Glue.

Now some of you are scratching your heads and wondering, "How does a person with an IQ higher than pastry get Super Glue in his EAR and not know it?" But you parents out there are no doubt nodding your heads and saying: "It would not surprise me to learn that this man has a three-year-old son."

And, of course, you're right. according to the AMA newsletter, the son "squirted the glue into the father's left ear while the man was sleeping." Fortunately surgeons were able to unclog the man's ear, but as medical consumers we can prevent this kind of near-tragedy by remembering to take these safety precautions:

1. Never keep three-year-old children around the house.
2. If you do, never sleep.

Also: You older children should remember that Super Glue is a serious household repair substance and NOT a toy to be used in such pranks as applying it to the toilet seats in the Faculty Men's Room, taking care to first prepare the surface by wiping it clean of oil and dirt.

Our next item was brought to our attention by Debbie and Lindsey Mackey, who alerted us to an article in the British medical journal the *Lancet* with the title:

"EXPLODING HEAD SYNDROME"

Quite frankly we were disappointed by this syndrome. We naturally assumed, from the title, that it would involve the actual explosion of a person's head, ideally Barry Manilow's in concert. But it turns out to be just this weenie syndrome where you wake up in the middle of the night having "a violent sensation of explosion in the head." Big deal. We get that all the time, but you don't see us whining to the *Lancet*. You see us making a mental note to drink gin from smaller containers.

But not right now. Right now we want to tell you about the exciting new:

ADVANCES IN B.O. MEASUREMENT

We found out about this through alert readers James McNab and Shelley Owens, who sent us an article from the *Journal of the American Society for Heating, Refrigera-*

tion and Air-Conditioning Engineers written by a man named—we are still not making this up—"P. Ole Fanger." Mr. Fanger, who hails from Denmark, has done a LOT of research in the field of measuring exactly how much a given human being tends to stink up a given room, and he has come up with a unit of air pollution called the "olf" ("from the Latin *olfactus,* or olfactory sense"). To quote the article: "One olf is the emission rate of air pollutants (bioeffluents) from a standard person (Figure 1)."

We sincerely wish that we could show you Figure 1, which is a truly wonderful drawing of a standard person with dozens of little Smell Arrows shooting out of his body. Looking at this drawing reminded us of one of the highlights of our life, which is the time that we were with two friends of ours, Randall and George, in a bar that was empty except for two women at the far end of the room, and George, after maybe 17 Miller High Lifes, decided to Make a Move, which was pretty funny because George, even on those occasions when he has total control over his dentures, is not exactly Paul Newman, or even Mr. Ed.

But he went lunging over there and, with all the subtlety of Hurricane Gilbert, attempted to strike up a conversation, which the two women were clearly not interested in. So they were quiet, and after a while George got quiet, and we were listening quietly, so the whole bar was very quiet when George had an unfortunate bodily event. It's the kind of event that can happen to anybody, except maybe Margaret Thatcher, but it rarely happens with the magnitude that it happened to George. You talk about Hurricane Gilbert. Of course, in those days we did not have modern measurement techniques, but we're sure that this event was completely off the scale on the Olf Meter. We're only sorry that we didn't get to see the two women virtually sprint from the bar, because we were lying flat on the floor laughing so hard that we thought we were going to suffer a heart attack, which every American should know the Six Warning Signs of.

TODAY'S MEDICAL TIP: Never undergo any kind of major surgery without first making an appointment.

ATTACK OF THE CARTOON ANIMAL HEADS

It's a Sunday evening, and we're driving home from Orlando, where we have taken our son, Robby, and his friend, Erik, for a special birthday weekend of fantasy and fun and hurling money at random around the Official Walt "You Will Have Fun" Disney Magical World of Theme Kingdoms and Resort Complex.

We're taking what the American Automobile Association has designated as the "scenic route" back to Miami, through south-central Florida, a region that used to cater primarily to frogs but that has in recent years sprouted dozens of "adult" (which we used to call "retired person") communities with names like Belle Harbour Vista Manour Downes Estates Centre West II, consisting of what we used to call "trailers," and later we called "mobile homes," and still later we called "manufactured houses." I don't know what we call them now. Probably something like "countrie townehome villas," as in "Hey, Ed! Lester's cow knocked over your countrie townehome villa again!"

We've been driving for three, maybe eight hours. In

the backseat, the boys have finished writing on their forearms with Official Walt Disney World souvenir felt-tipped markers, and are now passing the time with a little game they have invented with their soaring childhood imaginations: spitting on each other.

Ptooo, goes Robby.

Ptooo, goes Erik.

Ptooo, goes Robby.

This little game of saliva tennis is clearly audible in the front seat, but Beth and I, the Parental Authority Figures, say nothing. We are both thinking the same thing: *At least they are taking turns.* That is how low we have sunk on this car trip. We frankly would not mind

if they were back there shooting a high-powered rifle out the window, as long as they shared it. But, of course, they wouldn't.

"No fair!" Robby would shout. "Erik got three shots and I only got two but he won't give me back the rifle!" And Erik would say, "But Robby hit the farmer and I didn't hit anybody!" And Robby would say, "You did too! You hit the policeman!" And Erik would say, "Only his hat!" And finally one of us Authority Figures would whirl around and snap, "If you can't share the rifle, we're going to take it away and and then NOBODY WILL BE ABLE TO SHOOT ANYBODY."

We always get irritable like this when we return to harsh reality after a couple of days in Walt "You Are Having Some Fun Now, Yes?" Disney Resort and World and Compound, a place where your dreams really do come true, if you dream about having people wearing enormous cartoon-animal heads come around to your restaurant table and act whimsical and refuse to go away until you laugh with delight. This happens to you constantly at Disney World. I think it's part of a corporate discipline program for Disney executives. ("Johnson, your department is over budget again. You know what that means." "No! Please!" "Yes! *Into the Goofy suit!*")

We saw a lot of Goofy. Every time we sat down to eat, there he would be, acting whimsical. It got so that Robby and Erik, busily playing with their action figures, hardly even noticed him.

"Look, boys!" we would say, food dribbling down our chins. "Here comes Goofy! Again!"

Robby, not even looking up, would thrust one of his figures toward Erik and say: "This guy sends out a laser beam that can MELT YOUR EYEBALLS."

"Oh yeah?" Erik would say. "Well this guy makes a

noise like, mmmmmmPAAAAAH!, that goes through your ears and EXPLODES YOUR WHOLE HEAD."

Meanwhile, right behind them, encased in a heavy costume, this poor person, probably the executive vice president for group sales, would be writhing around, trying desperately to fulfill the boys' innocent childhood fantasies. Finally we grown-ups would have to let him off the hook. "Ha ha, Goofy!" we would say, speaking directly into the saltshaker, which is where we figured the microphone had been hidden by the Walt Disney World Whimsy Police. "You sure are causing us to laugh with delight!"

Don't get me wrong. I like Disney World. The rest rooms are clean enough for neurosurgery, and the employees say things like "Howdy, folks!" and actually seem to mean it. You wonder: Where do they get these people? My guess: 1952. I think old Walt realized, way back then, that there would eventually be a shortage of cheerful people, so he put all the residents of southwestern Nebraska into a giant freezer with a huge picture of Jiminy Cricket on the outside, and the corporation has been thawing them out as needed ever since.

Whatever the secret is, it works, and I urge you all to visit Disney World several dozen times. Afterward, I recommend that you drive down to Miami on the "scenic route," although if you notice two boys, ages 6 and 7, standing on the side of the road spitting at each other, my advice is not to pick them up.

DON'T BOX ME IN

We're moving again. We're not going far: Maybe two miles, as the heat-seeking radar-equipped South Florida Stealth Mosquito flies. It's hard to explain why we're doing this. Call it a crazy whim. We just woke up one morning and said, "I know! Let's put everything we own into boxes!"

And that's what we're doing. The giant cardboard mines of Peru are working overtime to meet our box needs, because we have a LOT of stuff that we need to take, including many precious heirlooms such as our calculator in which all the keys work perfectly except the "4," and our complete, mint-condition set of 1978 VISA statements (try replacing THOSE at today's prices). Stuffwise, we are not a lean operation. We're the kind of people who, if we were deciding what absolute minimum essential items we'd need to carry in our backpacks for the final, treacherous ascent to the summit of Mount Everest, would take along these aquarium filters, just in case.

The humorous part is, we never finished *unpacking*

from when we moved in here. The other day I watched my wife, Beth, as she opened a box that has been sitting around, unopened, since our last move, removed the contents, and carefully packed them, every last one, into a *new* box. I grant you that these are not the actions of a sane person, but you wouldn't be sane, either, if you'd spent the last few weeks doing what Beth has been doing, namely trying to get hold of workmen. The workmen are playing an elaborate prank wherein they come to our house and do a tiny smattering of work and then run off and hide in the Everglades for days at a time, breathing through hollow reeds and refusing to return Beth's phone calls. Every now and then one of them will come sneaking into our kitchen, frogs clinging to his hair, and shout, "nyah nyah nyah" at her, then sprint off before she can hurdle the boxes and grab him.

We need the workmen because we're trying to make our current house look domestic so that somebody will want to buy it. We're making a lot of simple, obvious improvements that never would have occurred to us to make while we actually lived here, because, tragically, we both happen to be domestically impaired. If we were birds, our nest would consist of a single twig with the eggs attached via Scotch tape. We lived for 11 years in a house with a light fixture that we both agreed was less attractive than if we had simply suspended a urinal from the ceiling. But of course we never did anything about it until we moved, just as in our current house we waited until now to clear out the giant tropical spiders who live next to the front door, subsisting on Federal Express men; or to replace the electrical ceiling-fan switch that has three positions, "Low," "Medium," and "Burn Down House"; or to eliminate the violently pink

carpet that made our bedroom look as though an Exxon tanker had run around there and spilled millions of gallons of Pepto-Bismol. Yes, we have plenty to do, and we're doing everything we can to attract workmen, including tying a string around a small bundle of money and placing it on the lawn as bait. When a workman approaches, we tug it slowly toward the house, and when he gets close enough we slam a box over him.

During this difficult time we have received a large mound of assistance from our two dogs. Using their keen, nearly asphalt-level intelligence, they have sensed that something important is happening, and have decided that their vital contribution will be to kill anybody who comes near our house. This means they have to spend a lot of time shut away in my office, barking. They've reached the point where they automatically start barking as soon as we shut them in there, whether or not there's anybody to bark at yet. It's their job, barking in my office. Somebody has to do it! They produce approximately one bark apiece every two seconds, so if I leave them in there for, say, 45 minutes, then open the door, I get knocked several feet backward by the escaping force of 2,700 accumulated barks.

Sometimes prospective buyers come to our house to look at it, and we have to go hide in the Everglades with the workmen. Buyers don't want you hanging around when they look at your house, because they feel free to make frank observations such as, "What are these? *Toenails?*" They would make this remark in my office, which contains many large unexplored toenail deposits that have built up over the years because I'm a professional writer, which means I spend as many as five hours a day engaged in foot maintenance while waiting for professional sentences to appear in my brain. But the rest of the house is looking real nice, thanks to Beth. In fact, she's starting to make me nervous: Yesterday she put some magazines on a table *in a fan arrangement.* This is of course one of the early symptoms of the dread June Cleaver Disease, which ultimately leads to the appearance, in your bathroom, of soap shaped like fruit. So I'm hoping we sell this house soon. Make us an offer. We're motivated. We're reasonable. We're accommodating. You get the dogs.

UN NINTENDED
BENEFITS

OK, I bought my child a Nintendo video-game system.
I realize I should not admit this. I realize the Child
Psychology Police may arrest me for getting my child a
mindless addictive antisocial electronic device instead of
a constructive old-fashioned educational toy such as an
Erector Set. Well let me tell you something: All my
childhood friends had Erector Sets, and although I am
not proud of this, I happen to know for a fact that, in
addition to the recommended educational projects such
as the Truck, the Crane, and the Carousel, it was possible to build the Bug Pulper, the Worm Extender, and
the Gears of Pain.

And speaking of pain, you have no idea how hard my
son made my life before I caved in and bought Nintendo. The technique he used was Power Wistfulness.
Remember the old comic strip "Dondi," starring the little syndicated orphan boy who always looked heart-
breakingly sad and orphanous and never got adopted,
possibly because he had eye sockets the size of manhole
covers? Well, my son looked like that. He'd start first

thing in the morning, standing around with Dondi-like eyes, emitting armor-piercing wistfulness rays and sighing over the fact that he was the only child outside of the Third World who didn't have Nintendo. Pretty soon I'd be weeping all over my toast, thinking how *tragic* it was—my own son, an orphan—until finally I just had to go to the Toys "Я" Approximately a Third of the Gross National Product store, because after all we're talking about a child's happiness here, and you can't put a price tag on . . . What? It cost HOW MUCH? What does it DO for that kind of money? Penetrate Soviet airspace?

No, really, it's worth every penny. I know you've

probably read a lot of articles by Leading Child Psychologists (defined as "people whose children probably wet the bed through graduate school") telling you why Nintendo is a bad thing, so let me discuss some of the benefits:

Benefit No. 1—Nintendo enables the child to develop a sense of self-worth by mastering a complex, demanding task that makes his father look like a total goober.

The typical Nintendo game involves controlling a little man who runs around the screen trying to stay alive while numerous powerful and inexplicably hostile forces try to kill him; in other words, it's exactly like real life. When I play, the little man becomes highly suicidal. If he can't locate a hostile force to get killed by, he will deliberately swallow the contents of a little electronic Valium bottle. So all my games end instantly, whereas my son can keep the little man alive through several presidential administrations. He is always trying to cheer me up by saying "Good try, Dad!" in the same sincerely patronizing voice that I once used to praise him for not getting peas in his hair. What is worse, he gives me Helpful Nintendo Hints that are far too complex for the adult mind to comprehend. Here's a verbatim example: "OK, there's Ganon and miniature Ganon and there's these things like jelly beans and the miniature Ganon is more powerfuller, because when you touch him the flying eagles come down and the octopus shoots red rocks and the swamp takes longer."

And the hell of it is, I know he's *right*.

Benefit No. 2—Nintendo strengthens the community.

One evening I got an emergency telephone call from our next-door neighbor, Linda, who said, her voice breathless with urgency: "Is Robby there? Because we just got Gunsmoke [a Nintendo game] and we can't get past the horse." Of course I notified Robby immediately. "It's the Liebmans," I said. "They just got Gunsmoke, and they can't get past the horse." He was out the door in seconds, striding across the yard, a Man on a Mission. Of course he got them past the horse. He can get his man all the way to the bazooka. *My* man dies during the opening credits.

Benefit No. 3—When a child is playing Nintendo, the child can't watch regular television.

Recently on the local news, one relentlessly personable anchorperson was telling us about the murder at a Pizza Hut, and when she was done, the other relentlessly personable anchorperson got a frowny look on his face, shook his head sadly, and said—I am not making this quotation up—"A senseless tragedy, and one that I am sure was unforeseen by the victims involved."

I don't want my child exposed to this.

Benefit No. 4—A child who is playing Nintendo is a child who is probably not burping as loud as he can.

I mention this only so I can relate the following true exchange I witnessed recently between a mother and her eight-year-old son:

SON: Burp. Burp. Burp. Burp. Bu . . .

MOTHER: Stop burping!

SON: But, Mom, it's my *hobby*.

So, Mr. and Ms. Child Psychologist, don't try to tell me that Nintendo is so terrible, OK? Don't tell me it makes children detached and aggressive and antisocial. In fact don't tell me anything. Not while the octopus is shooting these rocks.

LICKING THE
DRUG PROBLEM

What with the recent unsettling developments on the world political scene, particularly in the Middle East, I imagine that most of you are eager for a report on our yard.

We've moved to a new yard, which contains an alarming amount of nature. And I'm not talking about the friendly kind of yard nature that you get in, for example, Ohio ("The Buckeye State"), such as shrubbery and cute little furry baby buckeyes scampering around. I'm talking about the kind of mutant terroristic nature we get here in Florida ("The Assault Roach State"). For example, we have a kind of toad down here that, if you lick it, can kill you.

Now you're saying to yourself, "Yes, but who, aside from Geraldo Rivera seeking improved ratings, would lick a toad?" The answer is: More and more people. According to news articles that alert readers keep sending me, there's a brand of toad (not the kind here in Florida) that secretes a hallucinogenic substance when it

gets excited, and licking this toad has become a fad in certain circles. Which raises a couple of questions in my mind, such as: Does this occur in social settings? Do you have a group of sophisticated people sitting around a dinner table, finishing their coffee, and one of them reaches suavely into his jacket pocket, pulls out this thing that looks like a giant wart with eyeballs, and then, lowering his voice suggestively, says, "Anybody want to do some *toad*?" Also, how do they get the toad excited? Show it movies? Give it a tiny marital aid? Also, will Free Enterprise try to cash in on this? Will Anheuser-Busch come out with a TV commercial wherein some rugged-looking workmen, exhausted from a hard day of not showing up at people's houses, relax by taking some man-sized slurps off a Toad Lite?

Unfortunately I can't answer these questions, because I'm busy worrying about being killed by our mango tree. Our new yard has a mango tree, which I bet sounds like exotic fun to those of you who live in normal climates, right? Just think of it! All the mangoes you need, right in your own yard!

The problem is that, mangowise, you don't need a whole lot. You take one bite, and that takes care of your mango needs until at least the next presidential administration. But the mangoes keep coming. They're a lot like zucchini, which erupts out of the ground far faster than you could eat it even if you liked it, which nobody does, so you start lugging hundreds of pounds of zucchini to your office in steel-reinforced shopping bags, hoping your co-workers will be stupid enough to take some home, except of course they're lugging in their zucchini, all summer long, tons of it coming in, until the entire office building collapses in a twisted tangle of girders and telephone message slips and zucchini pulp, out of which new vines start to spring immediately.

Mangoes are even worse, because (a) they grow on trees, and (b) they're about the size of a ladies' bowling ball, only denser. They're the kind of fruit that would be designed by the Defense Department. They hang way up in our tree, monitoring the yard and communicating with each other via photosynthesis, and whenever they see me approaching they fire off a Warning Mango, sending one of their number thundering to Earth, cratering our lawn and alarming seismologists as far away as Texas ("The Silly Hat State"). Even on the ground, the mango remains deadly, because it immediately rots and becomes infested with evil little flies, and if you try to kick it off the lawn, it explodes, a mango grenade, covering your body with a repulsive substance known to botanists as "mango poop" that stays on your sneakers forever, so that when you go out in public, your feet are obscured by a cloud of flies, and the Florida natives snicker and say to each other, "Look! That idiot kicked a mango!"

So I keep a wary eye on the mango tree at all times, which means I am in constant danger of falling into the Scum Vat. This was originally intended to be a small decorative pool with maybe a couple of cute little goldfish in it, but at some point a gang of aggressive meat-eating algae took over. If you tried to put some goldfish in there, you'd never get close. A tentacle of algae would come swooping up and grab them out of your hand, and then you'd hear an algae burp. The only thing that can survive in there is the Giant Arguing Frogs. We've never actually seen them, but we hear them at night, when we're trying to sleep. They have a microphone hooked up to a 50,000-watt amplifier, and all night long they broadcast the following conversation:

FROG ONE: BWAAARRRRPPPP.

FROG TWO (disagreeing): BWAAARRRRPPPP.

You can tell they're never going to work it out. Some nights, lying in bed and listening to them, I've thought about going out there to mediate, but of course the algae would get me. You'd have to be some kind of dumb mango kicker to pull a stunt like that. Better safe than sorry, that's my motto, which is why I'd like to remind all my readers, especially you impressionable young people, that if you *must* lick a toad, make sure it's wearing a condom. Thank you.

A BRUSH
WITH GARDENING

It will probably come as no surprise to you that I got the idea of painting my lawn from an agency of the federal government.

When I say "painting my lawn," I don't mean my whole lawn. I just mean this one circular spot that suddenly, mysteriously turned brown, as though it had been visited by a small UFO or a large dog. I ignored the spot at first, but it started to grow, and I realized that it was similar to international communism: If you let it get a toehold in, say, Nicaragua, it will start to spread to the other strategic nations down there such as El Labrador and Costa "Ricky" Ricardo, and the next thing you know your entire lawn is brown.

So I was wondering what to do, when fortunately I received a letter from an alert reader named Dick Howard, who enclosed a news article from the *Roanoke* (Virginia) *Times and World News* about some National Forest Service rangers who painted a group of federal rocks to make them look more natural. I am not making this up. It happened in the Jefferson National Forest, where the

Forest Service had built a mountainside road that was designed, according to the article, "to blend in with the environment." It had a darkish color scheme, because, as you campers know, the environment consists primarily of dirt.

Unfortunately, there was an unscheduled flood, which exposed some large tacky white quartz rocks that frankly did NOT fit in with the natural road design. You can imagine how this offended the fashion sensibilities of the Forest Service personnel, who decided to do exactly what you would do if you were in charge of a national forest and had accidentally consumed a massive overdose of prescription medication: Paint the rocks. They did a few tests to select just the color they wanted, then they spent two days spraying paint on the rocks, and before you could say "massive federal budget deficit," the hillside looked just the way God would have created it if He had received the benefits of Forest Service training.

As a professional journalist, I have always been fascinated by people who appear to have even more spare time than I do, so I called up one of the men involved in the rock painting, District Ranger Bob Boardwine, who turned out to be a friendly individual. He told me that the rangers had taken a fair amount of ribbing over the rock-painting, but as far as he was concerned the project had come out real nice. I told him I was thinking about painting the brown spot on my lawn, and he gave me some fashion tips. "Make sure you use a dark green," he said. "When we painted the rocks, we went into it thinking in terms of a moss green and a light brown, but they weren't dark enough."

Thus advised, I asked my eight-year-old son if he wanted to help me paint the lawn, but he and his friend

Erik were deeply involved in an urgent Nintendo game that is not expected to be completed during my lifetime. Fortunately Erik's six-year-old brother, Tyson, was able to make some room in his schedule, so we got my son's watercolor set and went out to paint the brown spot. We were working on a blade-by-blade basis, and after a while we got tired of dark green, so at Tyson's suggestion we switched over to purple, then red, then orange, and when we were done we had converted what had been a dull and unattractive area of the lawn into an area that looked as though somebody had just thrown up several pounds of semi-digested jelly beans. Tyson and I were standing there admiring our work when—this really happened—up drove a pizza deliveryman, apparently sent by the God of Comedy Setup Lines.

"Looks like rain!" he said.

"Yes," I said, "and wouldn't you know it, I just painted my darned lawn!"

I added a friendly "Ha ha!" to reassure him I was a normal person unlikely to suddenly chop him into fragments with a machete, but he was already accelerating down the street. Nevertheless the lawn-painting was a critical success, and it got me thinking about other ways I might be able to improve nature around our house, especially the yard crabs. Since we live in South Florida, geologically a giant swamp with shopping centers, we have these crabs who live in holes in our yard, and I do not care for them. Being from the North, I prefer yard critters that are furry and cute, whereas crabs look like body parasites magnified 1,000 times. During mating season, they become outright hostile. I'll go out in my yard, and there, blocking my path, will be a crab, adopting a karate stance, and waving his pincers menacingly to prevent me from mating with his woman.

"I don't want to mate with your woman," I tell him. "Your woman is a *crab,* for God's sake." But this only makes him angrier, because I think he knows, deep inside his slimy little heart that I'm telling the truth.

So anyway, my idea is that the crabs should wear costumes. I'm thinking specifically chipmunk costumes. I could look out the window and watch them scuttling around the lawn in their furry finery, and it would be just like being back up North on a brisk fall day following a nuclear accident that had caused all the chipmunks to develop extra legs and walk sideways. My only question is where I'd get chipmunk costumes for crabs, but I'm sure the federal government can help me out. Assuming it's not too busy touching up federal rocks.

CAPTAINS OUTRAGEOUS

The reason we bought a motorboat is, we needed a new kitchen. Our current kitchen has a lot of problems, such as a built-in Colonial-era microwave that we think might not be totally safe because it can cook food that is sitting as far as 15 feet away. We had spent months striding around our current kitchen, making sweeping gestures and saying things like, "We'll move the sink over there!"

What a pair of goobers. As you experienced renovators know, it's easier to construct a major suspension bridge than to move a residential sink. Thousands of homeowners who embarked on sink-relocation projects during the Eisenhower administration are still washing their dishes in the bathtub. My wife and I kept running into people like this, people with plaster dust in their hair and hollow eyes from spending their wretched nights sleeping in the garage and their bleak days waiting desperately for workmen who inevitably made things worse. "We have no telephone or electricity or water," the Renovation People would say, "and on Monday a man is supposed to come and take all our oxygen."

This was discouraging, but we really needed a new kitchen. Finally we said, "OK, if we don't do it now, we're never going to do it," so we decided to bite the bullet and: Buy a motorboat. Our reasoning was, "Hey, if we have a motorboat, we'll have Family Outings where we can experience Togetherness and possibly crash into a reef and sink, and then it won't matter about our kitchen."

But reefs were not our immediate problem. Our immediate problem was something much worse, a daunting nautical challenge that has tested the courage of mariners since ancient times, namely: backing the boat into the carport. The trick to remember here is, if you turn your car wheels to the right ("starboard"), the boat trailer will actually go to the LEFT ("forecastle") until your wife ("Beth") announces that you ran over a sprinkler head ("$12.95"). Using this procedure I was able to get the boat into the carport in no more time than it took for Magellan to reach Guam.

We kept the boat moored in the carport for several weeks, after which we decided—call us bold adventurers—to try it on actual water. We met at the marina with our salesperson, Dale, who showed us how to launch the boat via a terrifying procedure wherein I had to back the trailer down a scary ramp right into the bay. I have since learned that, here in Miami, on weekends, amusement-seekers will come to the marina, set up folding chairs, and spend a highly entertaining day watching boat owners perform comical maneuvers such as forgetting to set their parking brakes and having their cars roll down the ramp and disappear, burbling gaily, below the surface. In the generous nautical tradition of rendering assistance to those in need, Miami boat owners sometimes—this is all true—get into gunfights over whose turn it is to use the ramp.

Fortunately we had Dale with us, so we had no trouble getting out on the water, where he taught me the basics of seamanship. Here's how it went:

DALE: OK, you see that shoal over there?

ME: No.

DALE: OK, you see that marker over there?

ME: No.

DALE: Do you want to take the wheel for a while?

ME: No.

Finally, when I was fully confident that, if necessary, I could take the boat out myself and get everyone killed, we returned home to spend a carefree evening washing our hull. You have to do this because it turns out that—get ready for a fascinating nautical fact—seawater is very bad for boats. I'm serious. Ask any boat owner. Seawater contains large quantities of barnacles and corrosives, which will rapidly turn your boat into a giant piece of maritime crud.

So while I was scrubbing my hull, I had this blinding insight: The smart thing to do, clearly, is never put the boat into the water. I shared this insight with some other boat owners, and they all agreed that, definitely, putting your boat into the water is asking for trouble. Most of them have had their boats sitting in their driveways long enough to be registered historical landmarks.

A group of us boat owners were discussing this one evening at a party featuring beer, which is how we decided to hold a Driveway Regatta. Really. I have the whole thing on videotape. We had it on our driveway, and we had four boats, on trailers, secured via anchors in the lawn, trees, etc. The judges awarded First Prize to a dentist named Olin, whose boat not only contained golf clubs and a croquet set, but also had a spider web containing a certified spider that had apparently died of old age. It was a fine afternoon, and nobody got seasick, and we even—try this at sea—had pizza delivered. I would have cooked, but we really need a new kitchen.

SHIP OF FOOLS

We wanted to have a relaxing family vacation, so we got together with two other families and rented a sailboat in the Virgin Islands. There is nothing as relaxing as being out on the open sea, listening to the waves and the wind and the sails and voices downstairs yelling "HOW DO YOU FLUSH THESE TOILETS?"

It takes a minimum of six people, working in close harmony, to successfully flush a nautical toilet. That's why those old ships carried such large crews. The captain would shout the traditional command—"All hands belay the starboard commode!"—and dozens of men would scurry around pulling ropes, turning giant winches, etc., working desperately to avoid the dreaded Backup At Sea, which is exactly the problem that the captain of the *Titanic* was downstairs working on, which is why he didn't notice the iceberg.

We had a competent captain in our cruise group, but just to be on the safe side we hired a local captain for the first afternoon to demonstrate the finer points of seamanship. He was on our boat for a total of three

Flushing
at
Sea

WATCH YOUR HEAD

hours, during which he demonstrated that he could drink six of our beers and two large direct-from-the-bottle swigs of our rum and still not fall headfirst into the Caribbean. He was definitely the most relaxed person on the boat. His major piece of nautical advice was: "No problem." We'd say: "Which Virgin Island is that over there?" And he'd squint at it knowledgeably and say, "No problem." Then he'd go get another beer.

So this was pretty much how we handled it, and the cruise was problem-free, unless you count my Brush With Death. For this I blame the children. We started the cruise with only five children, but after several days on the boat there appeared to be several hundred of them, all of whom always wanted to sit in exactly the same place, and no two of whom ever wanted to eat the same thing for lunch.

So one afternoon a group of them were playing an incredibly complex card game they had invented, wherein everyone had a different number of cards and anyone could change the rules at any time and punching was allowed and there was no possible way to end the game but everybody appeared to be winning, and suddenly a card blew overboard.

Until this kind of emergency arises, you never know how you're going to react. I happened to be nearby with a group of grown-ups who had smeared their bodies with powerful sun-blocking agents and then, inexplicably, gone out to lie in the sun, and when I heard the chilling cry ("Card overboard!") I leaped to my feet and, without thinking, in fact without any brain wave activity whatsoever, jumped into the water, dove beneath the surface, and saw: a barracuda the size of a nuclear submarine. The other people claimed it was only about three feet long, but I was right there, and this barracuda had actual torpedo tubes. It was examining the card closely, as if thinking, "Huh! A two of hearts, here in the Caribbean!" I used this opportunity to exit from the water by clawing violently at air molecules and ascending vertically, Warner Bros.–cartoon style, back into the boat.

Fortunately that was my only Brush With Death on the relaxation cruise, except for the other one, which occurred when I attempted to pull up the anchor. You have to pull up the anchor from time to time on a sailboat so that you can put up the sails, which causes the boat to lean over, which allows water to splash in and get all the clothes wet. It's a basic rule of seamanship that everybody's clothes have to be wet all the time. If there's no wind, you are required by maritime law to throw your clothes overboard a couple of times a day.

So I was standing on the deck, hauling up the anchor. You have to be careful on the deck, because of the "hatches," which are holes placed around a sailboat at random to increase the insurance rates. From the moment we got on the boat, I had been warning the children about the danger of falling into the hatches. "Don't fall into those hatches!" I'd say, in the stern voice that we wise old parents use to tell our children the ludicrously obvious. And so, as you have already guessed, when I was pulling on the anchor rope, walking backward, poof, I suddenly became the Incredible Disappearing Man. It was a moment of high relaxation, a moment that would definitely win the grand prize on the popular TV show "Boneheaded Americans Injure Themselves On Home Video," and I'm sure I'll have a good laugh about it once I'm out of surgery.

No, seriously, all I got was a bruise that is actually larger than my skin surface area, so that parts of it extend into the atmosphere around me. But other than that it was a swell cruise, and I strongly recommend that you take one. Make sure you go to the bathroom first.

DEATH
WORMED OVER

The key to a successful Summer Vacation Adventure is: preparation. For example, if you're planning a trip to Europe to visit historic sites such as the Hunchback of Notre Dame Cathedral, you should prepare *right now* by setting fire to your airline tickets. I'm advising against vacationing in Europe this year because Europe contains England, which is currently being invaded by the Alien Flatworms of Death.

I found out about this thanks to several alert readers who sent me a *Manchester Guardian* article that begins: "Killer flatworms from New Zealand which drug earthworms and devour them are invading Britain." The article quotes a scientist as saying: "They're weird; it is like something out of science fiction. They excrete an enzyme that paralyzes the worm like a narcotic drug. Then they excrete another one that dissolves the worm before your eyes like soup, then they suck it up. In about 30 minutes all that is left is a trace of old soil from the worm's stomach."

It is not definitely known how the killer flatworms got

from New Zealand to England. Possibly they smuggled themselves aboard a commercial airplane disguised as attorneys. We can only imagine what might have happened if they had become hungry en route:

FIRST AIRLINE PASSENGER: Have you seen Nigel?

SECOND AIRLINE PASSENGER: No, but what's this on his seat?

FIRST AIRLINE PASSENGER: Hey! That looks like Nigel's complimentary breakfast omelet!

You don't want this kind of tragedy to spoil your Vacation Adventure. So this year you should take an old-fashioned Family Fun Vacation, wherein you get into the family car and drive and drive and drive until

you come to an interesting local attraction, and then you drive past it at 78 miles per hour. I'm assuming here that Dad is driving. Dad likes to cover a lot of ground on a vacation. His ideal vacation itinerary would look like this:

6 to 6:15 A.M.—Eat breakfast.

6:15 to 6:30—Yellowstone National Park.

6:30 to 7—Canada.

And so on. Dad wishes he had auxiliary gas tanks so he could vacation all the way to, say, Argentina and back without ever stopping the car. Unfortunately, he has to refuel roughly every 600 miles, so sometimes Mom and the kids are able to escape and, running with their foreheads almost touching the ground because their bodies have been permanently molded into the shape of a car seat, flee into the underbrush in search of a local attraction.

For my money, the best attractions are small arts and crafts fairs. We once stopped at a fair in Pennsylvania Dutch country where a grim-looking woman was demonstrating how to make an authentic local dish from—this is true—the stomach of a pig. It was the scariest-looking thing I have ever seen that was not featured in a major motion picture, and the woman was gripping it with both hands, as if she were afraid that it might get loose and attack the other crafts. People would stop by, stare at it for a while, and ask, "What does it taste like?" And the grim-looking woman, not looking up, would reply, "A lot of people don't like it."

There are thousands of equally attractive attractions all over the country, but if you asked me, as a travel authority, which was No. 1, I would have to say it was the maggot races at the Town Club Bar in Three Forks, Montana. I am not making this up. Alert readers Bill and Julie Hudick sent me an article about it from the *Bozeman Daily Chronicle,* with a photograph of men hunched over a miniature racetrack, watching maggots race.

I immediately called the Town Club Bar and spoke to one of the people who conceived of this concept, Darrel Raffety, owner of Raffety's Fishbait Company, which sells maggots for bait. He explained that one day in the bar, a customer complained that there weren't enough maggots in the container he had bought, so they poured them out and counted them right on the bar, and some of the maggots (possibly disguised as attorneys) started crawling away, and suddenly, *eureka* (Greek, meaning "They probably had a few beers in them"), the maggot-racing idea was born.

So they held a race to raise money for charity, and it was a large success. Town Club Bar owner Phil Schneider told me he'd do it again if enough tourists come by and create a popular demand. So you will definitely want to include Three Forks in your summer vacation plans. Fortunately, it's only 357,000 miles from wherever you live. Dad is very excited.

THEY MIGHT BE
GIANTS

OK, fans. Time for Great Moments in Sports. The situation is this: The Giants are playing a team whose name we did not catch in the hotly contested Little League Ages 6 and 7 Division, and the bases are loaded. The bases are always loaded in this particular Division for several reasons.

First off, the coach pitches the ball to his own players. This is because throwing is not the strong suit of the players in the Ages 6 and 7 Division. They have no idea, when they let go of the ball, where it's headed. They just haul off and wing it, really try to *hurl* that baby without getting bogged down in a lot of picky technical details such as whether or not there is now, or has ever been, another player in the area where the ball is likely to land. Generally there is not, which is good, because another major area of weakness, in the Ages 6 and 7 Division, is catching the ball.

Until I became a parent, I thought children just naturally knew how to catch a ball, that catching was an instinctive biological reflex that all children are born

98

with, like knowing how to operate a remote control or getting high fevers in distant airports. But it turns out that if you toss a ball to a child, the ball will just bonk off the child's body and fall to the ground. So you have to coach the child. I go out in the yard with my son, and I give him helpful tips such as: "Catch the ball!" And: "Don't just let the ball bonk off your body!" Thanks to this coaching effort, my son, like most of the players on the Giants, has advanced his game to the point where, just before the ball bonks off his body, he winces.

So fielding is also not the strong suit of the Giants. They stand around the field, chattering to each other, watching airplanes, picking their noses, thinking about dinosaurs, etc. Meanwhile on the pitchers' mound, the coach of the opposing team tries to throw the ball just right so that it will bounce off the bat of one of his players, because hitting is another major area of weakness in the Ages 6 and 7 Division.

The real athletic drama begins once the opposing coach succeeds in bouncing the ball off the bat of one of his players, thus putting the ball into play and causing the fielders to swing into action. It reminds me of those table-hockey games, where you have a bunch of little men that you activate with knobs and levers, except that the way you activate the Giants is, you yell excitedly in an effort to notify them that the ball is headed their way. Because otherwise they'd probably never notice it.

"Robby!" I'll yell if the ball goes near my son. "The ball!" Thus activated, Robby goes on Full Red Alert, looking around frantically until he locates the ball, which he picks up and—eager to be relieved of the responsibility—hurls in some random direction. Then, depending on where the ball is headed, some other parent will try to activate his child, and the ball will be hurled again and again, pinball-style, around the field, before ultimately bonking off the body of the first baseman. Of course at this point the batter has been standing on the base for some time. Fortunately, in this league, he is required to stop there; otherwise, he could easily make it to Japan.

This is why the bases are always loaded, which is what leads us to today's Sports Moment. Standing on third base is James Palmieri, who is only 5, but who plays for the Giants anyway because his older brother, T.J., is on the team. James got on base via an exciting play: He failed to actually, technically, *hit* the ball, but the Giants' wily coach, Wayne Argo, employed a classic bit of base-

100

ball strategy. "Let's let James get on base," he said. And the other team agreed, because at this point the Giants were losing the hotly contested game by roughly 143–57.

So here it is: James is standing on third, for the first time in his entire life, thinking about dinosaurs, and next to him, ready to activate, is his mom, Carmen. And now Coach Wayne is throwing the pitch. It is a good pitch, bouncing directly off the bat. Bedlam erupts as parents on both teams try to activate their players, but none is shouting with more enthusiasm than Carmen. "Run, James!" she yells, from maybe a foot away. "Run!"

James, startled, looks up, and you can almost see the thought forming in his mind: *I'm supposed to run.* And now he is running, and Carmen is running next to him, cheering him on, the two of them chugging toward the plate, only 15 feet to go, James about to score his first run ever. Then suddenly, incredibly, due to a semirandom hurl somewhere out in the field, there appears, of all things: the ball. And—this is a nightmare—an opposing player actually *catches* it, and touches home plate and little James is OUT.

Two things happen:

- Carmen stops. "S-word," she says, under her breath. A mom to the core.
- James, oblivious, keeps running. Chugs right on home, touches the plate smiling and wanders off, happy as a clam.

You can have your Willie Mays catch and your Bill Mazeroski home run. For me, the ultimate mental picture is James and Carmen at that moment: the Thrill of Victory, the Agony of Defeat. A Great Moment in Sports.

━━━ READER ALERT ━━━

ENGLAND

I happen to like England a lot, and when I wrote this column, I thought it was clear that I was just poking some good-natured fun at one of our best international buddy countries. However, I got a lot of mail from angry Englishpersons, who made the following points:

1. I am a jerk.
2. The food in England isn't so bad.
3. What about the food at McDonald's?
4. England hasn't decapitated any members of royalty for a long time.
5. What about American crime?
6. Why don't I just shut up?
7. Boy, am I ever a jerk.

And so on. I was genuinely surprised by this hostile reaction, and all I can say to these people, in all sincerity, is: I humbly apologize for offending you, and I promise that I will never, ever again, even in jest, say anything remotely insulting about England, and I especially will not make note of the obvious defects in the royal gene pool.

BLIMEY!
FROGNAL COCKFOSTERS!

Recently my family and I spent a week in London, which is a popular foreign place to visit because they have learned to speak some English over there. Although frankly they have a long way to go. Often, when they get to the crucial part of a sentence, they'll realize that they don't know the correct words, so they'll just make some silly ones up. I had a lot of conversations that sounded like this:

ME: Excuse me. Could you tell us how to get to Buckingham Palace?

BRITISH PERSON: Right. You go down this street here, then you nip up the weckershams.

ME: We should nip up the weckershams?

BRITISH PERSON: Right. Then you take your first left, then you just pop 'round the gorn-and-scumbles, and, Jack's a doughnut, there you are!

ME: Jack's a *doughnut*?

BRITISH PERSON: Right.

Also they have a lot of trouble with pronunciation, because they can't move their jaw muscles, because of

103

malnutrition caused by wisely refusing to eat English food, much of which was designed and manufactured in medieval times during the reign of King Walter the Mildly Disturbed. Remember when you were in junior high school, and sometimes the cafeteria workers would open up a large Army-surplus food can left over from the Spanish-American War and serve you a scary-looking dish with a name like "Tuna Bean Prune Cabbage Omelet Casserole Surprise"?

Well, they still have a *lot* of food like that over in England, on permanent display in bars, called "pubs," where people drink for hours but nobody ever eats. We saw individual servings of pub food that we recognized from our last visit, in 1978. Some dishes—no effort is made to conceal this fact—contain *kidneys*. We also saw one dish with a sign next to it that said—I swear I am not making this up—"Spotted Dick."

The English are very good at thinking up silly names. Here are some actual stations on the London underground: Marylebone, Tooting Broadway, Piccadilly Circus, Cockfosters, Frognal, Goodge Street, Mudchute, Barking, and East Ham. Londoners are apologetic about their underground, which they believe has become filthy and noisy and dangerous, but which is in fact far more civilized than the average American wedding reception. At the height of rush hour, people on the London underground actually say "excuse me." Imagine what would happen if you tried an insane stunt like that on the New York City subway. The other passengers would take it as a sign of weakness, and there'd be a fight over who got to keep your ears as a trophy.

Our primary cultural activity in London was changing money. We had to do this a lot because the dollar is very weak. Europeans use the dollar primarily to apply shoe

polish. So every day we'd go to one of the money-chang-
ing places that are all over London, and we'd exchange
some dollars for British money, which consists of the
"pound" and a wide variety of mutant coins whose sizes
and shapes are unrelated to their values, and then we'd
look for something to eat that had been invented in this
country, such as pizza, and we'd buy three slices for
what we later realized was $247.50, and then we'd
change some money again. Meanwhile the Japanese
tourists were exchanging *their* money for items such as
Westminster Abbey.

In the interest of broadening our ten-year-old son's
cultural awareness, we visited some important historic

sites, including the Tower of London, the London Dungeon, and Madame Tussaud's Wax Museum, all of which are devoted to explaining in clinical detail how various historic members of royalty were whacked into small historic pieces. English history consists largely of royal people getting their heads chopped off, which is why members of the royal family now wear protective steel neck inserts, which is why they walk the way they do.

Needless to say, this brand of history was a hit with our son. He especially enjoyed the guided "Jack the Ripper" tour that we took one dark night with a very intense guide. "Right on this spot is where they found the victim's intestines," she'd say. "And right here is where they found the liver, which is now part of the food display of that pub over there."

Another cultural activity we frequently engaged in was looking the wrong way before attempting to cross streets. The problem is that in America, people drive on the *right* side of the street, whereas in London, they drive on *both* sides of the street, using hard-to-see cars about the size of toaster ovens. The best way to handle this, as a tourist, is to remain on one side of the street for your entire visit, and see the other side on another trip.

But I definitely recommend London for anybody who enjoys culture and could stand to lose a few pounds. I learned many things that will be of great value to me, not just personally, but also professionally, and I'm not saying that just to be polite to the English. I'm saying it because of Internal Revenue Service regulations.

DENTISTS
IN PARADISE

I want to stress that I did not go to Hawaii just to sit around the beach drinking giant comical drinks with names like the Wahine Martini that arrive at your table festooned with six kinds of fruit and a live parrot. No, I went to Hawaii for *sound journalism reasons.* Hawaii happens to be a hotbed of important news topics (FERDINAND MARCOS: HAS DEATH CHANGED HIM?), and as a trained journalist I felt it was my duty to "get the story," even though I knew I was running the very real risk that my entire trip would be tax-deductible.

First, some background. The Hawaiian Islands were discovered by hardy Polynesian sailors, who crossed thousands of miles of open ocean in primitive canoes, braving violent storm-tossed seas for months at a time. My family and I arrived by modern commercial aviation, which was infinitely worse. We flew on Halloween. "Never Fly on Halloween," this is my new aviation motto, because it took us 21 hours to get from Miami to Honolulu. We had two planes develop mechanical problems, one of them well out over the Pacific Ocean, which

is famous for not having places to land on. At one point, just before we took off from San Francisco for Honolulu the first time, the pilot—I am not making this up—said, "Hopefully, this one will fly all the way." Of course it didn't. The second time we took off from San Francisco, the flight attendant said, I swear, "If you gotta go, go with a smile." The flight was violently bumpy, and the movie was—this is still true—*The Dead Poets Society.* To apologize for all the inconvenience, the airline gave us coupons good for discounts on future flights, although they knew full well that we were all planning to return to the mainland via primitive canoe and never go near an airplane again.

But I don't want to dwell on the flight. I want to talk

about Hawaii, "The Aloha State." "Aloha" is an all-purpose Hawaiian phrase meaning "hello," "good-bye," "I love you," and "I wish to decline the collision damage waiver." The Hawaiian language is quite unusual because when the original Polynesians came in their canoes, most of their consonants were washed overboard in a storm, and they arrived here with almost nothing but vowels. All the streets have names like Kal'ia'iou'amaa'aaa'eiou, and many street signs spontaneously generate new syllables during the night. This confuses the hell out of the tourists, who are easily identifiable because they're the only people wearing Hawaiian shirts.

Things were very exciting when we were in Honolulu because the American Dental Association was holding a giant convention there. "Dentists in Paradise," is how I would describe it. There were 25,000 dental professionals wandering around, wearing shirts that appeared to be radioactive and looking at dental exhibits featuring large color illustrations of wonderful technical advances in dentistry that make you get down on your knees and pray they will never happen to you. I imagine the dentists probably also had some kind of large formal dental ceremony, where they gave out awards and took large ceremonial hits of nitrous oxide and drank a special wine toast and, in a solemn and moving tribute to those dental professionals no longer with us, spat the wine out into a giant ceremonial dental spittoon.

We missed this, but we did attend a "luau," which is Hawaiian for "a beach picnic featuring a large cooked pig who still has his eyeballs and stares at you while you're trying to eat him." Our pig's name was Bob. "Never eat anything that still has its eyeballs," that's my new culinary motto.

We also saw the famous Bonzai Pipeline, where brave or possibly just insane surfers ride on waves the size of Central American nations. My wife and son and I were standing on the beach, marveling at these waves, saying things like "Look at the SIZE of these waves! Look at this wave right HEEEAAAIIIEEEEE" and the next thing we knew we were being washed up the beach like the Jetsam Family, tourists in Full Bozo Mode.

This is why we were so wet when we ran into Imelda Marcos. This really happened. We were driving by the memorial park where Ferdinand was staying temporarily until Imelda could figure out a way to get him back to the Philippines, and we thought we'd stop and take a quick, unobtrusive gander. But when we got into Ferdinand's little private building, our shoes squishing as we walked, there was Imelda and her retinue. It was pretty awkward because they were dressed in full mourning attire and we were dressed like we just got off the Log Flume Ride at Disney World. Fortunately I am a trained journalist who knows how to handle himself in the presence of a major world figure. "Guck," I said, or some noise like it, way down in my throat, as I grabbed my son, who was wandering cheerfully over to the casket, and we squished the hell out of there. So I can't give you a detailed report on the Marcos situation, except to say that Ferdinand seems to be doing as well as can be expected, under the circumstances.

Satisfied that our trip now contained a very high percentage of business-related activity, we returned to Waikiki Beach, where we relaxed with a few tax-deductible drinks and watched the gorgeous sunset Pacific sky change colors behind the silhouettes of gently swaying dental professionals. Aloha. And I mean it.

THIS TAKES GUTS

Today we present the exciting results of a Scientific Taste Test that we ran recently here at the Institute of Scary Foods. This test was inspired by alert consumers Ken Weidner and Eric Simonson, who sent us a label from a canned food named—we are not making this up —"Armour Potted Meat Food Product." The ingredients listed on the label include: Beef Tripe, Beef Hearts, Cooked Fat Tissue Solids, and Partially Defatted Beef Fatty Tissue, which is always a popular family favorite ("Mom, I'd like another heaping mound of Partially Defatted Beef Fatty Tissue!")

Also on the label is a color picture labeled "SERVING SUGGESTION," which shows a brownish substance with parsley and an olive sitting on it. Here at the Institute of Scary Foods we are highly suspicious of olives, which, in our opinion, are the eyeballs of giant frogs. We believe that if you stood outside an olive factory, you'd hear the unmistakable tragic sound (RIBBETT-THUMP; RIBBETT-THUMP) of terrified sightless frogs leaping into things.

So we were not exactly insane about the Potted Meat Food Product label. However, our job is to keep you, the food-eating consumer, informed, so we called up the manufacturer's Consumer Information Center, where we spoke with a perky and helpful person named Barbara.

"What is 'beef tripe'?" we asked.

"Well, it's a part of the cow," said Barbara. "I'm trying to think of what part it is."

She put us on musical hold for a few minutes, then came back with a solid answer.

"The tripe is part of around the stomach area of the cow," she said.

Thus reassured, we set off for the convenience store. This is the same store where we once bought an amazing digital wristwatch that cost only $1.99, yet told the time. And when we say "the time," we mean it. If you set this watch at 2:14, it would keep saying "2:14" until you changed it to another time. This watch was so convenient that you didn't even have to wear it, because you always knew what it said.

Sure enough, this store had Armour Potted Meat Food Product, so we bought some, as well as *another* brand, Libby's Potted Meat Food Product. In addition to the beef tripe, the Libby's label says it contains pork stomachs, which could be a real selling point ("Now With TWO KINDS Of Stomachs!").

To round out our Taste Test, we purchased:
- A can of Spam;
- A can of Mighty Dog–brand dog food;
- A can of Bonton-brand "natural" snails;
- A can of something called "Beanee Weenees."

We also bought some tortilla chips, because we were concerned about an article we received from alert reader Stuart Ritter about a woman who ate an improperly chewed chip, which ripped a five-inch gash in her esophagus. The article quotes the woman's doctor as saying: "A poorly chewed tortilla chip can produce serious injury."

For the Taste Test, we offered the various food products to a five-member Expert Taste Panel, consisting of me; my wife, Beth; our son, Robert; our large main dog, Earnest; and our small emergency backup dog, Zippy. The results were as follows:
- Spam ranked highest, earning the title of "The Rolls-Royce Car Product of Canned Meat Products."

113

- The Potted Meat Food Products had the same appetizing look and texture of internal-organ-colored wood filler, but did not taste as good. They were definitely a cut below the Mighty Dog, which was grainy but at least tasted as though it had once been organic matter.
- Robert spat everything into the garbage except Spam and Beanee Weenees.
- Earnest licked everything a LOT and continued to lick the floor for several minutes after all detectable food molecules had disappeared.
- Nobody except Beth and Earnest would eat the snails, which look like little Jabba the Hutts and are clearly being sold as a prank.
- Zippy got so excited about the sudden unforeseen onslaught of food products that he had a little accident in the kitchen.

For safety reasons, we did not attempt to eat the Tortilla Chips of Doom. But we did establish, in a chilling experiment, that a single chip is capable of ripping a large, ugly gash in a personally computerized fund-raising letter we got from the Rev. Oral Roberts. Our advice to you consumers is: Don't try these experiments at home. Not without plenty of carbonated malt beverage product.

■■■■■ READER ALERT ■■■■■

DOGS

I've learned to live with the fact that my two dogs, Earnest and Zippy, are way more popular than I am. I always get a lot of mail when I write about them, and people are always asking me to write more, which is kind of puzzling inasmuch as all of my dog columns basically boil down to the following statement: "Boy, are dogs ever stupid!" Perhaps this reassures people. Perhaps they say, "Well, I may have missed out on that big promotion, and I may have screwed up my personal life, but at least I've never run headfirst into a tree at 37 miles per hour while chasing a squirrel. At least not while I was sober."

TAKING THE ZIP
OUT OF ZIPPY

I regularly get letters from irate MacNeil-Lehrer–watching readers who ask: "With all the serious problems facing the world, how come you write about your dogs?" To which I answer: Because I don't know anything about *your* dogs. Also—you can call me an idealist if you want, but this is my opinion—by writing about my dogs, I believe that I can bring my readers—rich and poor, young and old, intelligent and "lite"-beer drinking—to a greater awareness of, and appreciation for, my dogs. I want my dogs to someday be at least as famous as Loni Anderson. I want them to receive lucrative offers for major motion pictures based on their True Life Adventures.

This week, for example, our adventure is entitled:

ZIPPY AND EARNEST GET OPERATED ON

This adventure began when Zippy went through puberty, a biological process that a small dog goes through in less time than it takes you to throw away your Third

Class mail. One minute Zippy was a cute little-boy puppy, scampering about the house playfully causing permanent damage to furniture that is not yet fully paid for, and the next minute he was: A Man. When the new, mature version of Zippy sauntered into a room, you could almost hear the great blues musician Muddy Waters in the background, growling:

I'm a MAN
(harmonica part)
Yes I AM
(harmonica part)
A FULL-GROWN man.

Of course in Zippy's case, "full-grown" means "the

size of a Hostess Sno-Ball, yet somehow less impressive." But in his own mind, Zippy was a major stud muffin, a hunk of burnin' love, a small-caliber but high-velocity Projectile of Passion fired from the Saturday Night Special of Sex. And his target was: Earnest.

Earnest is a female dog, but she was not the ideal choice for Zippy, because all of her remotely suspicious organs had been surgically removed several years ago. Since that time she has not appeared to be even dimly aware of sex, or much of anything else. Her lone hobby, besides eating, is barking violently at nothing. Also she is quite large; when she's standing up, Zippy can run directly under her with an easy six inches of clearance. So at first we were highly amused when he started putting The Moves on her. It was like watching Tommy Tadpole hit on the Queen Mary.

But shortly the novelty wore off and we started feeling sorry for Earnest, who spent the entire day staring glumly off into dog hyperspace while this tireless yarnball-sized Lust Machine kept leaping up on her, sometimes getting as high as mid-shin, and emitting these presumably seductive high-pitched yips ("What's your sign? What's your sign?"). So we decided it was time to have the veterinarian turn the volume knob of desire way down on the stereo system of Zippy's manhood. If you get my drift.

The next morning Earnest was limping, so we decided to take both dogs to the vet. They bounded enthusiastically into the car, of course; dogs feel very strongly that they should always go with you in the car, in case the need should arise for them to bark violently at nothing right in your ear. When we got to the veterinarian's office they realized they had been tricked and went into

Full Reverse Thrust, but fortunately the floor material there is slippery enough to luge on. So when we last saw Zippy and Earnest that morning, they were being towed, all eight legs scrabbling in a wild, backward, futile blur, into: the Back Room.

When we picked them up that night, they were a pair of hurtin' cowpokes. Earnest, who had a growth removed, was limping badly, plus we had to put a plastic bag on her leg so she wouldn't lick her stitches off. And Zippy, to keep him from getting at *his* stitches, was wearing a large and very comical round plastic collar that looked like a satellite dish with Zippy's head sticking out in the middle. He had a lot of trouble getting around, because his collar kept hitting things, such as the ground.

For the next week, if you came to our front door, here's what happened: You heard the loud barking of two dogs going into Red Alert mode, but you did not see any immediate dogs. Instead you heard a lot of bumping and clunking, which turned out to be the sound of a large dog limping frantically toward you but suffering a major traction loss on every fourth step because of a plastic bag, combined with the sound of a very small dog trying desperately to keep up but bonking his collar into furniture, doorways, etc. And then, finally, skidding around the corner, still barking, there appeared the dynamite duo: Bagfoot and Satellite Head.

During this week we were not the least bit worried about burglars, because if anyone had tried to break into our house, we would have found him the next morning, lying in a puddle of his own drool. Dead from laughter.

YELLOW JOURNALISM

If you were to ask me, "Dave, what are the two words that summarize everything that you truly believe in, other than that beer should always be served in a chilled glass?" I would have to respond: "Dog obedience." I own two dogs, and they have both been trained to respond immediately to my voice. For example, when we're outside, all I have to do is issue the following standard dog command: "Here, Earnest! Here, Zippy! C'mon! Here, doggies! Here! I said come HERE! You dogs COME HERE RIGHT NOW!! ARE YOU DOGS LISTENING TO ME?? HEY!!!" And instantly both dogs, in unison, like a precision drill team, will continue trotting in random directions, sniffing the ground.

This is of course exactly what I want them to do. Dogs need to sniff the ground; it's how they keep abreast of current events. The ground is a giant dog newspaper, containing all kinds of late-breaking dog news items, which, if they are especially urgent, are often continued in the next yard. We live next to an aircraft-carrier-sized dog named Bear, who is constantly committing acts of prize-winning journalism around the neighborhood, and my dogs are major fans of his work. Each morning, while I am shouting commands at them, they race around and scrutinize the most recent installments of the ongoing Bear *oeuvre,* vibrating their bodies ecstatically to communicate their critical comments ("Bear has done it AGAIN!" "This is CLASSIC Bear!" etc.).

Of course you cannot achieve this level of obedience overnight. You have to take the time to understand dogs as a species, to realize that they have not always been peaceful domesticated animals who fulfill their nutritional requirements primarily by sidling up to the coffee table when you're not looking and snorking taco chips directly out of the bowl. Millions of years ago dogs were fierce predators who roamed in hungry packs; if some unfortunate primitive man got caught out in the open, the dogs would surround him, knock him to the ground, and, with saliva dripping from their wolflike jaws, lick him to within an inch of his life. "Dammit, Bernice!" he would yell to primitive woman. "We got to get these dogs some professional obedience training!" This is still basically the situation today.

We had our larger dog, Earnest, professionally trained by a very knowledgeable woman who came to our house and spent several hours commanding Earnest to "heel." Wouldn't it be funny if it turned out that animals actually had high IQs and understood English perfectly, and the only reason they act stupid is that we're always giving them unintelligible commands? Like, maybe at night in the stable, the horses stand around asking each other: "What the hell does 'giddyap' mean?"

But the trainer had no trouble getting Earnest to comprehend "heel." Her technique was to give commands in a gentle but firm voice; to consistently praise Earnest for obeying properly; and to every now and then, as a reminder, send 75,000 volts of electricity down the leash. At least that's how I assume she did it, because in no time she had Earnest heeling like Vice President Quayle. Whereas when *I* take Earnest for a "walk" I am frequently yanked horizontal by dog lunges of seminuclear force—Earnest could tow a bulldozer across Nebraska—so that my body, clinging desperately to the leash, winds up bouncing gaily down the street behind Earnest at close to the federal speed limit, like a tin can tied to a newlywed couple's car.

But "heel" is not the only obedience skill our dogs have mastered. They also know:

ANSWER THE DOOR—When a person, real or imagined, comes to our house, both dogs charge violently at the front door barking loudly enough to shatter glass, because they know, through instinct, that there is a bad guy out there and they *must protect the house.* So when we open the door, no matter who is standing there—a neighbor, a delivery person, Charles Manson holding a four-foot machete—the dogs barge *right past him* and race outside, looking for the bad guy, who for some reason is never there, a mystery that always causes the dogs to come to skidding four-legged stops and look around with expressions of extreme puzzlement. Foiled again! He's a clever one, that bad guy!

GO TO SCHOOL—The highlight, the absolute pinnacle, of our dogs' entire existence is riding in the car when we drive our son to school, an activity that gives them the opportunity to provide vital services such as barking at policemen and smearing dog snot all over the rear window. So every morning they monitor us carefully, and the instant we do something that indicates to them that our departure is imminent, such as we wake up, they sprint to the garage door and bark at it, in case we've forgotten where it is, then they spring back to us and bark some more, to let us know they're ready to go, and then they spring back to the garage door, then back to us, and so on, faster and faster, until they become barely visible blurs of negative-IQ canine activity rocketing through the house at several hundred revolutions per minute, and you can just imagine how difficult it can be for us to make them understand the concept of "Saturday." One nonschool morning my wife felt so sorry for them that she went out in her bathrobe and drove them around the neighborhood for a while, looking for things they could bark at. So don't try to tell me dog training isn't worth it, OK? I can't hear you anyway, because there's a bad guy at the door.

JUST SAY NO
TO RUGS

Everybody should have a pet. And I'm not saying this just because the American Pet Council gave me a helicopter. I'm also saying it because my family has always owned pets, and without them, our lives would not be nearly so rich in—call me sentimental, but this is how I feel—dirt.

Pets are nature's way of reminding us that, in the incredibly complex ecological chain of life, there is no room for furniture. For example, the only really nice furnishing we own is an Oriental rug that we bought, with the help of a decorator, in a failed attempt to become tasteful. This rug is way too nice for an onion-dip-intensive household like ours, and we seriously thought about keeping it in a large safe-deposit box, but we finally decided, in a moment of abandon, to put it on the floor. We then conducted a comprehensive rug-behavior training seminar for our main dog, Earnest, and our small auxiliary dog, Zippy.

"NO!!" we told them approximately 75 times while looking very stern and pointing at the rug. This proven

training technique caused them to slink around the way dogs do when they feel tremendously guilty but have no idea why. Satisfied, we went out to dinner.

I later figured out, using an electronic calculator, that this rug covers approximately 2 percent of the total square footage of our house, which means that if you (not you *personally*) were to have a random diarrhea attack in our home, the odds are approximately 49 to 1 against your having it on our Oriental rug. The odds against your having *four* random attacks on this rug are more than *five million to one*. So we had to conclude that it was done on purpose. The rug appeared to have been visited by a group of specially bred, highly trained Doberman Poopers, but we determined, by interrogating both dogs, that the entire massive output was the work of Zippy. Probably he was trying to do the right thing. Probably, somewhere in the Coco Puff–sized nodule of nerve tissue that serves as his brain, he dimly remembered that The Masters had told him *something about the rug*. Yes! That's it! *To the rug!*

At least Zippy had the decency to feel bad about what he did, which is more than you can say for Mousse, a dog that belonged to a couple named Mike and Sandy. Mousse was a Labrador retriever, which is a large enthusiastic bulletproof species of dog made entirely from synthetic materials. This is the kind of dog that, if it takes an interest in your personal regions (which of course it does) you cannot fend it off with a blowtorch.

So anyway, Mike and Sandy had two visitors who wore expensive, brand-new down-filled parkas, which somehow got left for several hours in a closed room with Mousse. When the door was finally opened, the visibility in the room had been drastically reduced by a raging down storm, at the center of which was a large quivering down clot, looking like a huge mutant duckling, except that it had Mousse's radiantly happy eyes.

For several moments Mike and Sandy and their guests stared at this apparition, then Mike, a big, strong, highly authoritative guy, strode angrily into the room and slammed the door. He was in there for several minutes, then emerged, looking very serious. The down clot stood behind him, wagging its tail cheerfully.

"I talked to Mousse," Mike said, "and he says he didn't do it."

People often become deranged by pets. Derangement is the only possible explanation for owning a cat, an animal whose preferred mode of communication is to

127

sink its claws three-quarters of an inch into your flesh. God help the cat owner who runs out of food. It's not uncommon to see an elderly woman sprinting through the supermarket with one or more cats clinging, leech-like, to her leg as she tries desperately to reach the pet-food section before collapsing from blood loss.

Of course for sheer hostility in a pet, you can't beat a parrot. I base this statement on a parrot I knew named Charles who belonged to a couple named Ed and Ginny. Charles had an IQ of 260 and figured out early in life that if he talked to people, they'd get close enough so he could bite them. He especially liked to bite Ed, whom Charles wanted to drive out of the marriage so he could have Ginny, the house, the American Express card, etc. So in an effort to improve their relationship, Ginny hatched (ha ha!) this plan wherein Ed took Charles to—I am not making this up—Parrot Obedience School. Every Saturday morning, Ed and Charles would head off to receive expert training, and every Saturday after-noon Ed would come home with chunks missing from his arm. Eventually Ginny realized that it was never going to work, so she got rid of Ed.

I'm just kidding, of course. Nobody would take Ed. Ginny got rid of Charles, who now works as a public-relations adviser to Miss Zsa Zsa Gabor. So we see that there are many "pluses" to having an "animal friend," which is why you should definitely buy a pet. If you act right now, we'll also give you a heck of a deal on a rug.

THINGS THAT
GO HORNK
IN THE NIGHT

These are indeed exciting times we live in, what with the radical political changes in Eastern Europe, the dramatic developments in South Africa, and of course the long-overdue Illinois Owl Vomit Study. This was alertly brought to my attention by reader Paul Baker, who sent an article from the *Wisconsin State Journal* headlined LAWMAKERS CHOKE ON OWL VOMIT STUDY. It seems that some Illinois legislators are upset because the state is funding a $180,000 study wherein researchers go around collecting owl vomit to see what they (the owls) eat, which could have important implications.

"Owls spit up pellets of hair, bone, and teeth . . . at least once or twice a day," states the article.

This is also true of our small auxiliary dog, Zippy. His hobby is throwing up lizard parts when we're trying to eat dinner. He'll get that look of total concentration that dogs get when they have a really important task to perform, then he'll hunch his body over and walk around in a circle making a noise that sounds like "hornk." If you put him outside, he'll sit patiently by the door until you let him back inside, then he'll resume hornking. "Never throw your lizard parts up outside" is Rule No. 1 of the Dog Code of Ethics.

So as you can imagine our dinners have a very appetizing ambience:

MY WIFE: Would you like some more stew?

ME: Sure, I'd love . . .

ZIPPY: Hornk.

ME: On second thought . . .

ZIPPY: HORRRRNNK.

MY SON: Look! A tail and a leg!

ME: I think I'll just lie down.

And I'll tell you something else that is not helping my

appetite any: Our refrigerator currently contains a jug of pond water infested with mosquito larvae, which are so unappetizing as to make semi-digested lizard parts look like Chicken McNuggets. The reason we have mosquito larvae in our refrigerator, as you parents have already deduced, is that our son is doing a science-fair project, which involves seeing what happens to larvae when you put them into various environments such as the refrigerator environment, the hall-closet environment, etc. Here are our key findings:

1. In the hall-closet environment, the larvae turn into mosquitoes and wait in the dark until you open the door, when they hurl their little bodies pathetically up against the side of the jar and, with their whiny little voices, go, "PLEASE let me out please please PLEASE I won't suck your blood I SWEAR." But they are lying.

2. In the refrigerator environment, the larvae do nothing, and after a while you don't even notice them, leading to the danger that their jar will become part of the general population of Mystery Refrigerator Items like the leftover takeout Chinese food from the Carter administration, and then one day Grandpa Bob will come to visit, and in the middle of the night he'll get thirsty and tiptoe out to the refrigerator, reach in, pull out what looks like a nice refreshing jug of iced tea, take a big swig and GAAAAAACCCCCKKKK thud to the floor. And then Zippy will throw up on him.

But I will say this for our dogs: They never shot anybody. This is more than I can say for the dog in Lyngdal, Norway, that shot a man. According to a news article sent in by many alert readers, the man was hunting rabbits, and he set his gun down, and his dog "accidentally" hit the trigger, causing the gun to go off. Fortunately, the man suffered only minor injuries. Unfortunately, the rabbits saw the whole thing and have obtained a mail-order assault rifle.

Just kidding, of course! But I am NOT kidding about the Arson Cat. According to an Associated Press story also alertly sent in by numerous readers, investigators concluded that a house fire in Lima, New York, was caused by "a cat playing with matches," prompting us to once again ask ourselves, as concerned citizens, WHEN the government is going to come to its senses and order the mandatory sterilization of ALL cat owners.

On a brighter note, the *New Zealand Herald* reports that a woman in Adelaide, Australia, received a hefty out-of-court settlement "after she was hit in the back by an eight-kilogram frozen tuna during the world tuna-tossing championships." The story adds that the organizers of this annual event "are now trying to make the sport safer for spectators by developing a rubber tuna."

So there is Hope for Tomorrow. In fact, things are looking better already: Alert reader Perry Bradshaw sent me a news item stating that the governor of Minnesota, whose name (I am not making this governor up) is "Rudy Perpich," has declared 1990 to be "The Year of the Polka." I wouldn't be surprised if this exciting event drew music enthusiasts from as far away as Illinois ("The Owl Vomit State"). I'd be there myself, but I have to taunt the hall-closet mosquitoes.

━━━━ READER ALERT ━━━━

EAT BUGS FOR MONEY

I got hundreds of responses to this column, including dozens from people who were willing to eat bugs for free. Bear in mind that, under our system of government, these people can vote.

━━━━━━━━━━━━━━━━━━━

BEETLEJUICE

There comes a time in the life of every American citizen when Duty calls. "Hey! YOU!!" are Duty's exact words, and unless you're some kind of flag-desecrating pervert, you're going to stand up, as Americans have stood up for more than 200 years, and you're going to say, "Yes, I will participate in the Arbitron television-ratings survey."

I answered The Call one recent afternoon. The phone rang, and it was a person informing me that I had been selected to be an Arbitron household based on an exhaustive screening process consisting of being home when my number was dialed at random. As you can imagine, I was deeply moved.

"Do I get money?" I asked.

The reason I asked this is that a couple of years ago I was a Nielsen-ratings household, and all they paid me was two lousy dollars, yet they wanted me to write down *every program I watched,* which was virtually impossible because I'm a guy and therefore I generally watch 40 programs at once. Guys are biologically capable of keep-

ing track of huge numbers of programs simultaneously by changing the channel the instant something boring happens, such as dialogue. Whereas women, because of a tragic genetic flaw, feel compelled to watch only *one program at a time,* the way people did back in the Middle Ages, before the invention of remote control.

Anyway, it turns out that $2 is also all you get for being an Arbitron household. But I agreed to be one anyway, because, let's face it, when anybody connected with the television industry asks you to do something, no matter how stupid or degrading it is, you do it. This is why people are willing to openly discuss their secret bodily problems in commercials that are seen by the entire nation. These people become *famous* for having secret bodily problems. When they go out to dinner, large celebrity-worshiping crowds gather to stare and point and whisper excitedly to each other, "Look! It's Elston V. Quadrant, Hemorrhoid Sufferer!"

At least these people get paid, which is more than you can say for the people who go on the syndicated TV talk show and seek to enhance public understanding of various tragic psychological disorders by candidly revealing that they are total wackmobiles ("I'm Geraldo Rivera, and these men are commercial-airline pilots with live trout in their shorts").

So I figured the least I could do, for television, was be an Arbitron household. This involves two major responsibilities:

1. Keeping track of what you watch on TV.

2. Lying about it.

At least that's what I did. I imagine most people do. Because let's face it: Just because you watch a certain show on television, that doesn't mean you want to *admit* it. Let's say you're flipping through your 8,479 cable channels, and you come across a program called "Eat Bugs For Money," wherein they bring out a large live insect, and the contestants secretly write down the minimum amount of money they would have to be given to eat it, and whichever one has the lowest bid has to actually do it. Admit it: YOU would watch this program. In fact, right now you're saying to yourself, "Hey, I wonder what channel that's on." Unfortunately, at present it's still in the conceptual stage. It's based on an idea from my editor, Gene Weingarten, who has publicly stated that he would eat a live adult South Florida cockroach (average weight: 11 pounds) for $20,000.

My point is that you'd watch this program, but you wouldn't tell Arbitron. You'd claim that you watched a *National Geographic* special with a name like "The Amazing World of Beets." In my Arbitron diary, I wrote that our entire household (including Earnest, who is, legally, a dog) mainly watched the network news, whereas in fact the only remotely educational programming we watched that week was a commercial for oat bran, which by the way is clearly no more intended for human consumption than insects are.

Speaking of which, here is a Late Bulletin: My wife— this is the wonderful thing about Free Enterprise—has considered Gene Weingarten's bid and announced that *she* would eat a live adult cockroach for just $2,000. If you sincerely feel you can beat that price, drop me a line c/o The Miami Herald, Miami, FL 33132, because I'd like to produce a pilot episode of "Eat Bugs For Money" with an eye toward—call me a Cultural Pioneer—advancing the frontiers of my income. I would also appreciate your lowest price on eating a nonpoisonous but hair-covered spider. Thank you.

SKIVVYING UP
THE PROFITS

Recently—I bet this has happened to you—I ran out of clean underwear in Los Angeles. So I wandered into the men's clothing department of an upscale department store, the kind of store where the salesclerks all have sharp haircuts and perfectly tailored suits that are far nicer than anything YOU own, and, although they act very deferential, you know they're secretly watching to see which clothes you touch so they can have them burned later as a precaution against vermin.

So I was skulking around, looking for the underwear section, and I came across the Ralph Lauren Exhibit, which, in addition to clothes, featured an old saddle, croquet mallets, and various other props associated with rich people. Ralph uses these to create a fashion look that has made him several zillion dollars, a look that I would describe as "Wealthy Constipated WASP." His magazine advertisements feature Lauren-clad people with their hair slicked back, standing around in large antique-infested houses, looking grim, as if they have just received the tragic news that one of their key polo ponies had injured itself trampling a servant to death and would be unavailable for an important match.

I myself am of WASP heritage, and although my family was not even close to wealthy, we knew WASPs who were, and I frankly cannot understand why any fun-oriented person would want to imitate their life-style. Wealthy WASPs have less fun in their entire lifetimes than members of other ethnic groups have at a single wedding reception. Trust me. I have been to both WASP and non-WASP weddings, and your WASP couple can get married, go on their honeymoon, came home, pursue careers, have children, and get divorced in less time than it takes for a non-WASP couple to get

THIS ⊙☆#! T-SHIRT HAS THIS STUPID HORSE ON IT, WHICH MEANS I BOUGHT IT FOR $57.50

to the part of their reception where everybody drinks champagne from the maid of honor's brassiere.

Nevertheless, the WASP look has been very good to Ralph Lauren. So has another clothing line of his that I would describe as "Pretend Cowboy," which is advertised via photographs of rugged male models, wearing designer cowboy outfits and authentic Wild West male fragrances, fixin' to ride their tastefully color-coordinated horses down to the Old Tradin' Post to purchase a heap o' stylin' gel.

So anyway, I was looking at the Lauren Exhibit, and I came across this T-shirt. It was a regular white T-shirt such as you might use to mow the lawn in or mop up spilled Yoo-Hoo with, except for two things:

1. On the front, in large letters, it had the words RALPH LAUREN STATE FAIR SEPT. 26–OCT. 1 and a large picture of a cowboy on a horse that was bucking wildly (perhaps because the cowboy was wearing too much male fragrance).

2. The price was $57.50.

Yup. Fifty-seven dollars and fifty cents. I once bought an entire *suit* for less than that. I admit that it was not an elegant suit. It was made from what appeared to be the same material they use to cover mattresses. I think it actually had a tag on the lapel that could not be removed under Penalty of Law. I was afraid to wear this suit late at night for fear that tired people would try to lie down on me. (Rim shot.) But at least it was a whole suit, for less than Ralph charges for a *T-shirt*.

Not that I mean to be critical. Hey, people are *buying* these things, just as they are paying top dollar for jeans that appear to have been ripped to shreds by crazed wolverines. You know why? Because garments like these make a *statement.* You wear a Lauren State Fair T-shirt,

140

and you are telling the world: "I paid $57.50 for this T-shirt. God alone knows what I would pay for an official Ralph Lauren jockstrap."

So I am all in favor of the designer T-shirt concept, and I am only sorry that the Lauren Exhibit didn't feature any men's briefs for $38.95 per leg hole, or whatever Ralph would charge. I wound up having to go elsewhere and purchase another famous designer underwear brand. A French one. Le Mart du K.

ROTTEN TO
THE CORE

You residents of rustic, tractor-intensive regions such as Ohio will be pleased to hear that New York City has decided to become polite. Really. There's a new outfit called New York Pride, which is attempting to get New Yorkers to at least pretend that they don't hate everybody. This program resulted from a survey in which researchers asked tourists how come they didn't want to come back to New York, and the tourists said it was because there was so much mean-spiritedness. So the researchers spat on them.

No, seriously, I think New York is very sincere about this. I was in the city recently, and right off the bat I noted that the Teenage Mutant Ninja Taxi Driver who took me to the hotel was very thoughtfully allowing pedestrians as much as .3 nanoseconds to get out of his way, which many of them graciously did even though a taxi does not, technically, have the right-of-way on the sidewalk. The driver was also careful to observe the strict New York City Vehicle Horn Code, under which it is illegal to honk your horn except to communicate one of the following emergency messages:

1. The light is green.
2. The light is red.
3. I hate you.
4. This vehicle is equipped with a horn.

Even very late at night, when there were probably only a few dozen vehicles still operating in the entire city, they'd all gather under my hotel window every few minutes to exchange these vital communications.

Another example of politeness I noticed was that nobody ridiculed my clothes. Everybody in New York, including police horses, dresses fashionably, and whenever I'm there, even in my sharpest funeral-quality suit with no visible ketchup stains, I feel as though I'm wearing a Hefty trash bag. And it's *last year's* Hefty trash bag.

On this trip I also became paranoid about my haircut. After 20 years of having the same haircut, I recently got a more modernistic style that's a little longer in the back, and I was feeling like one hep "dude" until I got to New York, where the fashionable guys all had haircuts in which the hair is real long on top, but abruptly stops halfway down the head, forming a dramatic Ledge of Hair that depressed lice could commit suicide by jumping from. Nobody has had my haircut in New York since 1978. Pigeons were coming from as far away as Staten Island to void themselves on it. But the New Yorkers themselves politely said nothing.

Aside from this courtesy epidemic, the other big story in New York is that—get ready for a Flash Bulletin—the United Nations *still exists*. Yes! Like you, I thought

that the UN had been converted to luxury condominiums years ago, but in fact it's still there, performing the vital function that it was established to perform in this troubled, turmoil-filled world: namely, hold receptions.

In fact, using the advanced journalism technique of having a friend give me his invitation, I was able to get into a reception hosted by the U.S. ambassador, who is, in my candid assessment, a tall man named "Tom" with a lot of armed guards. After shaking hands with Tom, I proceeded into the reception area, which was filled with representatives of nations large and small, rich and poor, from all over the world; and although I sometimes tend to be cynical, I could not help but be deeply moved, as a journalist and a human being, by the fact that some of these people had haircuts *even worse than mine*. This was particularly true of the Eastern Bloc men, who looked as if they received their haircuts from the Motherland via fax machine.

But the important thing was, everyone had a good time. People would arrive filled with international tension, but after several drinks and a couple of pounds of shrimp, they'd mellow right out, ready to continue the vital UN work of going to the next reception.

I decided that, since I was there, I might as well use proven journalism techniques to find out if any World Events were going on. So I conducted the following interview with a person standing next to me:

ME: So! Who are you?

PERSON: I'm a [something about economics] from [some country that sounded like "Insomnia"].

ME: Ah! And how are things there?

PERSON: Better.

ME: Ah! (Pause.) What continent is that in, again?

Unfortunately at that point the person had to edge away, but nevertheless I had what we journalists call the "main thrust" of the story, namely: Things are better in Insomnia. It was definitely a load off my mind, and as I walked out into the brisk New York evening, I experienced a sense of renewed hope, which was diminished only slightly by the knowledge that taxis had been sighted in the area, and I would never make it back to the hotel alive.

WELL ENDOWED

Obscenity. Pornography. Naked people thrusting their loins. Should these things be legal? What is obscenity? What is art? What exactly are "loins"? How come nobody ever calls the office and says: "I can't come to work today because I have a loinache"? These are some of the serious questions that we must ask ourselves, as Americans, if we are going to get away with writing columns about sex.

These issues are relevant right now because of the raging national debate over the National Endowment for the Arts, which was established to spend taxpayers' money on art, the theory being that if the taxpayers were allowed to keep their money, they'd just waste it on things they actually wanted. Because frankly, the average taxpayer is not a big voluntary supporter of the arts. The only art that the average taxpayer buys voluntarily either has a picture of Bart Simpson on it or little suction cups on its feet so you can stick it onto a car window.

So if you left it up to the public, there would be hardly

any art. Certainly there would be no big art, such as the modernistic sculptures that infest many public parks. You almost never hear members of the public saying, "Hey! Let's all voluntarily chip in and pay a sculptor upwards of $100,000 to fill this park space with what appears to be the rusted remains of a helicopter crash!" It takes concerted government action to erect one of those babies.

The taxpayers also cannot be relied upon to support performing arts such as opera. As a taxpayer, I am forced to admit that I would rather undergo a vasectomy via Weed Whacker than attend an opera. The one

time I did sit through one, it lasted approximately as long as fourth grade and featured large men singing for 45 minutes in a foreign language merely to observe that the sun had risen.

My point is that the government supports the arts for the same reason that it purchases $400,000 fax machines and keeps dead radioactive beagles in freezers: Nobody else is willing to do it. The question is, should we carry this concept further? Should the government require taxpayers not only to pay for art, but also to go and physically admire it? This program could be linked with the federal court system:

JUDGE: Mr. Johnson, you have been convicted of tax evasion, and I hereby sentence you to admire four hours of federally subsidized modern dance.

DEFENDANT: NO! NOT MODERN DANCE!!

JUDGE: One more outburst like that, Mr. Johnson, and I'm going to order you to also watch the performance artist who protests apartheid using a bathtub full of rigatoni.

So federal art is good. But now we must grope with the troubling question: Should the government support smut? And how do we define "smut"? You can't just say it's naked people, because many famous works of art, such as the late Michelangelo's statue of David getting ready to fight Goliath, are not wearing a stitch of clothing. Which raises the question: Why would anybody go off to fight in the nude? Was it a tactic? Perhaps this explains why Goliath just stood there like a bozo and let himself get hit by a rock. "Hey!" he was probably thinking. "This guy is naked as a jaybird! What's he trying to AWWRRK."

Some people argue that a work is not pornographic as long as it has redeeming social value. But you can

148

find people who will testify in court that almost anything has redeeming social value:

PROSECUTOR: So, Professor Weemer, you're saying that this video depicts an ecology theme?

WITNESS: Yes. The woman displays a LOT of affection for the zucchini.

On the other end of the spectrum, some people think that just about everything is evil. For example, the Reverend Donald Wildmon, a leading anti-pornography crusader, once mounted a crusade against a Mighty Mouse cartoon. I swear I am not making this up. In this cartoon, Mighty Mouse took a whiff of something; the cartoon makers said it was clearly flower petals, but the Reverend Wildmon was convinced that Mighty Mouse was snorting cocaine.

Of course it's difficult to believe that Mighty Mouse, even if he is a cocaine user, would be stupid enough to snort it on camera. But, as parents, we have to ask ourselves: What if the Rev. Wildmon is right? And speaking of cartoon characters with apparent drug problems, how come Donald Duck has been going around for 50 years wearing a shirt but no pants? Flashing his loins! Right in front of Huey, Dewey, and Louie, his so-called nephews, if you get my drift! And consider this: If you call up the Walt Disney public relations department, they'll tell you that Mickey and Minnie Mouse are not married, despite having the same last name. Come to think of it, they also have "nephews."

My point is that the obscenity-art issue involves many complex questions, and we owe it to ourselves, as Americans, to give them some serious thought. You go first.

PRANKS
FOR THE MEMORIES

I love Halloween. And not just because it gives us a chance to buy a new mailbox. No, what I love most is the fun of opening our front door and hearing a group of costumed youngsters happily shout out the traditional Halloween greeting: "(Nothing)."

At least that's what traditionally happens at our house. The youngsters just stand there, silent. They have no idea that I have opened the door. They are as blind as bats, because their eyes are not lined up with the eyeholes in their costume masks.

Poorly aligned eyeholes are an ancient Halloween tradition, dating back at least as far as my childhood in Armonk, New York. My early Halloween memories consist of staggering around disguised as a ghost, unable to see anything except bed sheet, and consequently bonking into trees, falling into brooks, etc. The highlight of my ghost career came in the 1954 Halloween parade, when I marched directly into the butt of a horse.

Today's children, of course, do not wear bed sheets. They wear manufactured costumes representing li-

censed Saturday-morning cartoon characters and purchased from the Toys "Я" A Billion-Dollar Industry
store, but I am pleased to note that the eyeholes still
don't line up. So when I open the door on Halloween, I
am confronted with three or four imaginary heroes
such as G.I. Joe, Conan the Barbarian, Oliver North,
etc., all of whom would look very terrifying except that
they are three feet tall and facing in random directions.
They stand there silently for several seconds, then an
adult voice hisses from the darkness behind them: *"Say
'Trick or Treat,' dammit!"*

This voice of course belongs to good old Dad, who
wants more than anything to be home watching the

World Series and eating taco dip in bulk, but who must instead accompany the children on their trick-or-treat rounds to make sure I don't put razor blades in the candy. This is a traditional Halloween danger that the local perky TV news personalities warn us about every year, using the Frowny Face they put on when they have to tell us about Bad News, such as plane crashes and rainy weekends.

So I understand why good old Dad has to be there, but he makes me nervous. I can feel him watching me suspiciously from somewhere out there, and I think to myself: What if he's armed? This is a reasonable concern, because I live in South Florida, where *nuns* are armed. So I am very careful about the way I hand out treats.

"Well, boys or perhaps girls!" I say to the licensed characters, in a voice so nonthreatening as to make Mr. Rogers sound like Darth Vader. "How about some NICE CANDY in its ORIGINAL PACKAGING that you can clearly see when I hold it up to the porch light here has NOT BEEN TAMPERED WITH?" Alerted by the sound of my voice, the licensed characters start lurching blindly toward me, thrusting out trick-or-treat bags already containing enough chocolate to meet the nation's zit needs well into the next century.

Of course there is more to Halloween than massive carbohydrate overdoses. There is also the tradition of bitching about pumpkin prices, a tradition that my wife and I enjoy engaging in each year after paying as much as $20 for a dense inedible fruit so that some pumpkin rancher can put a new Jacuzzi in his Lear jet. This is followed by the tradition of scooping the insides, or, technically, the "goop," out of the pumpkin, a chore that always falls to me because both my wife and son refuse to do it, and not without reason, what with the alarming increase in pumpkin-transmitted diseases. (Get the facts! Call the American Pumpkin Council! Don't mention my name!)

But I consider the risk of permanent disfigurement to be a small price to pay for the excitement that comes when I finally finish carving Mr. Jack O'Lantern and put him out on the front porch, there to provide hours of pleasure for the trick-or-treating youngsters except that (a) they can't see and (b) Mr. Jack O'Lantern immediately gets his face kicked into mush by older youngsters playing pranks.

Pranks—defined as "activities that struck you as truly hilarious when you were a teenager but, now that you are a property owner, make you wish you had a high-voltage fence"—are another ancient Halloween tradition. The first Halloween prank ever, played by a group of Druid teenagers, was Stonehenge ("HEY! You kids GET THOSE ROCKS OFF MY LAWN!!"). I can't really complain about the pranks, because as a youth I played several thousand myself. In fact, I figure there must be a God of Prank Justice, who keeps track of everything we do when we're young and then uses Halloween to settle the score ("OK, that's his 14th mailbox. He has 57 to go."). Vastly enjoying this spectacle, I bet, are the ghosts of all my former victims. Assuming they can see through their eyeholes.

SILENT NIGHT, HOLY %*&?c

The Holiday Season is here again, and there's "something special" in the air. It's the aroma being given off by our mailperson, who expired in our driveway several days ago while attempting to deliver 300 pounds of Holiday Greeting cards. These were mostly from businesses sending us heartfelt pre-printed bulk-mailed holiday wishes like:

> *'Tis now a time for Peace on Earth*
> *And Joy for all Mankind*
> *So let us know if we can help*
> *Unclog your sewer line.*

But we don't have time to read all our holiday wishes. We're too busy engaging in traditional holiday activities such as Setting Up the Electric Train That Doesn't Work. I bought this train set for my son on his first Christmas, when he was two months old and the only way he knew to play with it was by putting it in his mouth. So it developed some kind of serious train disorder, probably drool in the motor, and every year, when we finally get it hooked up and plugged in, it just sits there, humming. The Little Engine on Valium.

But we can't spend too much time playing with the train, because we have to get on with the tradition of Replacing All the Bulbs in the Christmas Tree Lights. We save big money by buying very inexpensive lights that were manufactured by Third World residents who have no words in their language for "fire code." These lights use special bulbs that are designed to stand up under virtually any kind of punishment except having electricity go through them. If the train isn't humming too loud, we can actually hear the bulbs scream when we plug them in, telling us it's time once again to troop down to the drugstore, where we spend approximately $14,000 per holiday season on replacement bulbs, many of which have been pre-burned-out at the factory for our holiday convenience.

But we can't spend too much time enjoying our tree, because we have to get down to the mall to watch the traditional and highly competitive Holiday Shoppers' Hunt for One of the Four Remaining Department Store Salesclerks in North America. "Ho ho ho!" we shout as a clerk is flushed out of Housewares and makes a desperate dash through Small Appliances, pursued by a baying pack of holiday shoppers, slashing the air with sharpened VISA cards.

Jingle bells! Jingle bells! sings Mister Low-Fidelity Mall Loudspeaker as loud as he can right in our ear. He sings it over and over and over, because he knows it's the kind of traditional holiday song that we can listen to for an entire nanosecond without growing tired of it. *Jingle bells!* it goes. *Jingle BELLS! Jingle BELLS, DAMMIT! JINGLE BANG . . .*

Uh-oh! It looks like Mr. Low-Fidelity Mall Loud-

speaker has been shot by another important holiday tradition, the Increasingly Desperate Guy Shopper. He's trying to find something for that Special Someone in his life, who has made it clear that this year she'd like something a little more personal than what he got her last year, which was a trailer hitch. So he's edging warily through the aisles of what is, for guys, a very dangerous section of the department store, a section where sometimes women wearing scary quantities of makeup lunge out from behind pillars and spray you with fragrances with names like Calvin Klein's Clinical Depression. All around are potential gift items, but there's no way for the guy shopper to tell which ones would be thoughtful and appropriate, and which ones would cause that Special Someone to place an urgent conference call so she could inform all her friends simultaneously what a bonerhead she is hooked up with.

Last holiday season I went to a department store with a friend of mine named Joel, who was trying to buy something for Mary. He became badly disoriented in the scarf section, which featured a display of tiny fragile cloth wisps that had no imaginable function and that cost as much per wisp as a radial tire. It looked to me like some kind of holiday prank, but Joel, rapidly losing brain function from breathing a department-store atmosphere that was 2 parts oxygen and 17 parts cologne, grabbed one basically at random and actually *bought* it. But that was not his major gift purchase. His major gift purchase was something totally romantic, something that represents the ultimate in traditional holiday gift giving: a jogging bra. I am not making this up. "She'll love it!" he said. I agreed, but only because I knew that if he didn't finish shopping soon he'd start throwing money directly into wastebaskets.

Speaking of which, I need to get my holiday butt over to the Toys Sure "Я" Expensive Considering How Fast They Break store before they run out of Giant Radioactive Nose Worms from Space or whatever popular heavily advertised holiday toy concept my son is hoping Santa will bring him. I doubt that Santa will to come to our house personally this year. The reindeer would go berserk if they got a whiff of the mailperson.

GARBAGE SCAN

Monday morning. Bad traffic. Let's just turn on the radio here, see if we can get some good tunes, crank it up. Maybe they'll play some some early Stones. Yeah. Maybe they . . .

—POWER ON—

". . . just reached the end of 14 classic hits in a row, and we'll be right back after we . . ."

—SCAN—

". . . send Bill Doberman to Congress. Because Bill Doberman agrees with us. Bill Doberman. It's a name we can trust. Bill Doberman. It's a name we can remember. Let's write it down. Bill . . ."

—SCAN—

". . . just heard 19 uninterrupted classic hits, and now for this . . ."

—SCAN—

". . . terrible traffic backup caused by the . . ."

—SCAN—

. . . EVIL that cometh down and DWELLETH amongst them, and it DID CAUSETH their eyeballs to

ooze a new substance, and it WAS a greenish color, but they DID not fear, for they kneweth that the . . ."

—SCAN—

". . . followingisbasedonan800-yearleaseanddoesnotincludetaxtags-insuranceoranactualcarwegetyour-houseandyourchildrenandyourkidneys . . ."

—SCAN—

"NINE THOUSAND DOLLARS!!! BUD LOOTER CHEVROLET OPEL ISUZU FORD RENAULT JEEP CHRYSLER TOYOTA STUDEBAKER TUCKER HONDA WANTS TO GIVE YOU, FOR NO GOOD REASON . . ."

—SCAN—

". . . Bill Doberman. He'll work for you. He'll *fight* for you. If people are rude to you, Bill Doberman will *kill* them. Bill Doberman . . ."

—SCAN—

". . . enjoyed those 54 classic hits in a row, and now let's pause while . . ."

—SCAN—

". . . insects DID swarm upon them and DID eateth their children, but they WERE NOT afraid, for they trustedeth in the . . ."

—SCAN—

". . . listening audience. Hello?"

"Hello?"

"Go ahead."

"Steve?"

"This is Steve. Go ahead."

"Am I on?"

"Yes. Go ahead."

"Is this Steve?"

—SCAN—

"This is Bill Doberman, and I say convicted rapists have *no business* serving on the Supreme Court. That's why, as your congressman, I'll make sure that . . ."

—SCAN—

". . . a large quantity of nuclear waste has been spilled on the interstate, and police are trying to . . ."

—SCAN—

". . . GIVE YOU SEVENTEEN THOUSAND DOLLARS IN TRADE FOR ANYTHING!!! IT DOESN'T EVEN HAVE TO BE A CAR!!! BRING US A ROAD KILL!!! WE DON'T CARE!!! BRING US A CANTALOUPE-SIZED GOB OF EAR WAX!!! BRING US . . ."

—SCAN—

"... huge creatures that WERE like winged snakes EXCEPT they had great big suckers, which DID cometh and pulleth their limbs FROM their sockets liketh this, 'Pop,' but they WERE not afraid, nay they WERE joyous, for they had ..."

—SCAN—

"... just heard 317 uninterrupted classic hits, and now ..."

—SCAN—

"Bill Doberman will shrink your swollen membranes. Bill Doberman has ..."

—SCAN—

"... glowing bodies strewn all over the road, and motorists are going to need ..."

—SCAN—

"... FORTY THOUSAND DOLLARS!!! WE'LL JUST GIVE IT TO YOU!!! FOR NO REASON!!! WE HAVE A BRAIN DISORDER!!! LATE AT NIGHT, SOMETIMES WE SEE THESE GIANT GRUBS WITH FACES LIKE KITTY CARLISLE, AND WE HEAR THESE VOICES SAYING ..."

—SCAN—

"Steve?"

"Yes."

"Steve?"

"Yes."

"Steve?"

—SCAN—

"Yes, and their eyeballs DID explode like party favors, but they WERE NOT sorrowful, for they kneweth ..."

—SCAN—

Bill Doberman. Him good. Him heap strong. Him your father. Him ..."

—SCAN—

". . . finished playing 3,814 consecutive classic hits with no commercial interruptions dating back to 1978, and now . . ."

—SCAN—

". . . the radiation cloud is spreading rapidly, and we have unconfirmed reports that . . ."

—SCAN—

". . . liquefied brain parts did dribbleth OUT from their nostrils, but they WERE not alarmed, for they were . . ."

—SCAN—

". . . getting sleepy. Very sleepy. When you hear the words 'Bill Doberman,' you will . . ."

—POWER OFF—

OK, never mind. I'll just drive. Listen to people honk. Maybe hum a little bit. Maybe even, if nobody's looking, do a little singing.

(Quietly)
I can't get nooooooo
Sa-tis-FAC-shun . . .

WHERE YOU CAN
STICK THE
STICKER PRICE

We are attempting to purchase a new car, and I have just one teensy little question: WHY WON'T THEY TELL YOU HOW MUCH IT COSTS?

I mean, let's say you're in the market for a rutabaga. You go to the supermarket and there, plain as day, is a sign stating the price of the rutabaga, allowing you to decide instantly whether it is in your price range. If it is, you simply pay the amount and take your rutabaga home, and you hurl it into your garbage disposal. At least that's what I would do, because I hate rutabagas.

But when you walk into a car dealership, you are entering Consumer Hell. There is no easy way to find out what the actual true price of any given car is. Oh, sure, there is a "sticker price," but only a very naive fungal creature just arrived from a distant galaxy would dream of paying this. In fact, federal law now requires that the following statement appear directly under the sticker price:

WARNING TO STUPID PEOPLE:
DO NOT PAY THIS AMOUNT.

The only way to find out the real price is to undergo a fraternity-style initiation. First you squint at the sticker, which lists the car's 163 special features, none of which you could ever locate on the actual car because they all sound like rocket parts, as in "transverse-mounted induced-torque modality propounders." Then a salesperson comes sidling toward you in an extremely casual fashion (do not attempt to escape, however; an experienced car salesperson can sidle great distances at upwards of 45 miles per hour) and chatters on at length about the many extreme advantages of whatever car you are looking at ("It has your obverse-shafted genuine calfskin bivalve exuders"). But if you ask him the true price, he will make some vague, Confucius-type statement like: "Dave, we are definitely willing to go the extra mile to put a smile on your face."

"But how much does it cost?" you say.

"Dave," he says, lowering his voice to indicate that you and he have become close personal friends. "Frankly, Dave, (name of whatever month it is) has been a slow month, and I think, Dave, that if we sit down and cut bait, we can come up with a number that we can play ball with."

"WHAT number?" you say. "TELL ME THE NUMBER."

"Dave," he says, "I think if we both pull on our oars here, we can put the icing on the cake while the iron is still hot."

The easiest solution, of course, is to simply pull out a loaded revolver and say, "Tell me how much this car costs or I will kill you," but unfortunately it is still a misdemeanor in some states to shoot a car salesperson. So eventually you have to start *guessing* at the price ("Is it more than $9,500?"). It is very similar to the childhood game Twenty Questions, only it takes much longer, because instead of saying "yes" or "no," the salesperson always answers: "Let me talk to my manager."

The manager is comparable to the Wizard of Oz, an omnipotent being who stays behind the curtain and pulls the levers and decides whether or not the Cowardly Lion will get a free sunroof. I have never heard a conversation between a manager and a salesperson, but I assume it goes like this:

SALESPERSON: He wants to know if it's more than $9,500. Can I tell him?

MANAGER: How many times have you called him "Dave"?

SALESPERSON: 1,672 times.

MANAGER: Not yet.

So it can take hours to determine the true price, and this is just for one car. If you want to find out the price of another brand of car, you have to go through the entire fraternity initiation all over again. And there are hundreds of brands of cars out there. *Thousands* of them. Back when I was a child and Abraham Lincoln was the president, there were only about four kinds of cars, all of them manufactured by General Motors, but now you see new dealerships springing up on a daily basis, selling cars you never heard of, cars whose names sound like the noise that karate experts make just before they break slabs of concrete with their foreheads ("Hyundai!!").

So far, the cars we have looked at include: the Mimosa Uhuru 2000-LXJ. The Mikado Sabrina Mark XVIXMLCM, and the Ford Peligroso, which is actually the same as the Chevrolet Sombrero, the Jeep Violent Savage, and the Chrysler Towne Centre Coupe de Grace, and which is manufactured partly in Asia (engine, transmission, body) and partly in the United States (ashtray). They are all fine cars, but at the present time, based on our discussions with the various salespersons, we find ourselves leaning toward the rutabaga.

LEMON HARANGUE

TODAY'S CONSUMER TOPIC IS:
How to Buy a Car.

The First Rule of Car Buying is one that I learned long ago from my father, namely: Never buy any car that my father would buy. He had an unerring instinct for picking out absurd cars, cars that were clearly intended as industrial pranks, cars built by workers who had to be blindfolded to prevent them from laughing so hard at the product that they accidentally shot rivets into each other.

For example, my father was one of the very few Americans who bought the Hillman Minx, a wart-shaped British car with the same rakish, sporty appeal as a municipal parking garage but not as much pickup. Our Minx also had a Surprise Option Feature whereby the steering mechanism would disconnect itself at random moments, so you'd suddenly discover that you could spin the wheel all the way around in a playful circle without having any effect whatsoever on the front wheels. Ha ha! You can imagine how I felt, as an insecure 16-year-old with skin capable of going from All-Clear Status to Fully Mature Zit in seconds, arriving at the big high school pep rally dance, where all the cool guys had their Thunderbirds and their GTOs with their giant engines and 23 carburetors, and there I was, at the wheel of: the Hillman Minx. A car so technologically backward that the radio was still receiving Winston Churchill speeches.

You don't see many Minxes around anymore, probably because the factory was bombed by the Consumer Product Safety Commission. You also don't see many Nash Metropolitans, another car my father bought. The Metropolitan was designed by professional cartoonists to look like the main character in a children's book with a name like *Buster the Car Goes to Town*. It was so small that it was routinely stolen by squirrels. It was not the ideal car for dating, because there was room for only one person, so the other one had to sprint along the side of the highway, trying to make casual conversation and sometimes dropping from exhaustion. Being a gentleman, I always made sure my dates carried flares so I could go back and locate them at night.

Of course today's cars are much more sophisticated, by which I mean "expensive." This is because modern cars employ all kinds of technologically advanced concepts such as measuring the engine in "liters." Let's say you buy a car with a "5.7-liter engine": This means that when it breaks, you should not ask your mechanic how much it's going to cost until you've consumed 5.7 liters of a manufacturer-approved wine.

The most important consideration, in buying a new car, is the rebate. This is one area of automotive technology where America still reigns supreme. A lot of

Japanese cars don't even *have* rebates, whereas some American car dealerships have become so sophisticated that *they no longer even sell cars.* You just go in there and sign legal papers for a couple of hours and get your rebate and your zero-percent financing with no payments due until next Halloween, and you drive home in your same old car. Ask your automotive sales professional for details. He's clinging to your leg right now.

NO! JUST KIDDING! The last time I jokingly suggested that there was anything even slightly unpleasant about buying a car, several million automotive sales professionals wrote me letters threatening to take all their advertising out of the newspaper and jam it up my

nasal passages. So let me state in all sincerity that as far as I am concerned these people are gods, and car-buying is the most legal fun that a person can have while still wearing underwear.

But it can also be confusing. There are so many brands of cars today, with new ones constantly being introduced, not only from domestic manufacturers but also from foreign countries such as Mars. I refer here to the "Infiniti," a car that was introduced by a bizarre advertising campaign in which—perhaps you noticed this—*you never actually saw the car*. Really. All you saw in the magazine ads was ocean waves, leading you to wonder: Is this a submersible car? Or was there some kind of accident during the photo session? ("Dammit, Bruce, I TOLD you the tide was coming in!")

But no, the Infiniti ads were done that way on purpose. They wanted you to spend $40,000 on this car, plus whatever it costs to get the barnacles off it, but they *refused to show it to you*. Why? Because the Infiniti is actually: the *Hillman Minx*.

No, just kidding again. The truth is that the Infiniti ads are part of an exciting new trend called "Advertising Whose Sole Purpose Is to Irritate You." The ultimate example of this is the magazine ads for Denaka vodka, where a haughtily beautiful woman is staring at you as though you're the world's largest ball of underarm hair, and she's saying, "When I said vodka, I meant Denaka." What a fun gal! I bet she's a big hit at parties. ("*Pssst!* Come into the kitchen! We're all gonna spit in the Denaka woman's drink!")

My point is that there's more to buying a car than just kicking the tires. You have to really know what you're doing, which is why, all kidding aside, I recommend that you carefully analyze your automotive needs, study the market thoroughly, and then purchase the car that you truly feel, in all objectivity, has the most expensive advertisement in this newspaper. Don't thank me: I'm just keeping my job.

TRAFFIC INFRACTION, HE WROTE

Probably the greatest thing about this country, aside from the fact that virtually any random bonerhead can become president, is the American system of justice. We are very fortunate to live in a country where every accused person, unless he has a name like Nicholas "Nicky the Squid" Calamari, is considered innocent until such time as his name appears in the newspaper. Also you have the constitutional right (the so-called Carmen Miranda right) to be provided—at the taxpayers' expense, if you cannot afford one—with an enormous fruit-covered hat. But the most important right of all is that every criminal is entitled to a Day In Court. Although, in my particular case, it occurred at night.

Let me stress right out front that I was as guilty as sin. I was driving in downtown Miami, which in itself shows very poor judgment because most Miami motorists graduated with honors from the Moammar Gadhafi School of Third World–Style Driving (motto: "Death Before Yielding").

So I probably should never have been there anyway,

and it served me right when the two alert police officers fired up their siren, pulled me over, and pointed out that my car's registration had expired. I had not realized this, and as you can imagine I felt like quite the renegade outlaw as one of the officers painstakingly wrote out my ticket, standing well to the side of the road so as to avoid getting hit by the steady stream of passing unlicensed and uninsured motorists driving their stolen cars with their left hands so their right hands would be free to keep their pit bulls from spilling their cocaine all over their machine guns.

Not that I am bitter.

When he gave me the ticket, the officer told me that

I had to appear in court. I had never done this before, so I considered asking my attorney, Joseph "Joe the Attorney" DiGiacinto, to represent me. Unfortunately, Joe is not a specialist in traffic matters, in the sense that —and I say this as a friend—he is the worst driver in the history of the world. I figured he might not be the ideal person to have on my side in traffic court:

JOE: Your Honor, my client . . .

JUDGE (interrupting): Wait a minute. Aren't you Joseph DiGiacinto?

JOE: Um, well . . .

JUDGE: The person who had driver licenses revoked by *three different states?*

JOE: *Well, I . . .*

JUDGE: The person who once, during a crowded street festival in New York's colorful Chinatown district, attained a speed of almost 45 miles per hour on the *sidewalk?*

JOE: Well, yes.

JUDGE: I sentence your client to death.

So I thought I'd be better off representing myself. I've watched "The People's Court" for years, and I pride myself on my ability to grasp the issues involved, even in complex cases involving highly technical points of law such as, does the dress shop have to take back the defective formal gown if the buyer got B.O. stains on it. In fact, I have always secretly wanted to be a lawyer. I could picture myself in a major criminal case, getting the best of my opponent through clever verbal sparring and shrewd courtroom maneuvers:

ME: So, Mr. Teeterhorn, you're telling us that you "can't recall" why you happened to bring a flame-thrower to the bridge tournament?

WITNESS: That's right.

ME: Well, perhaps THIS will help refresh your memory.

WITNESS: NO! GET THAT THING AWAY! OUCH!! IT'S BITING ME!!!

OPPOSING ATTORNEY: I object, Your Honor! Mr. Barry is badgering the witness!

ME (coolly): Your Honor, as these documents clearly prove, Rex here is a wolverine.

JUDGE (examining the documents): OK, I'll allow it.

By the night of my traffic court appearance, I had worked out a subtle yet crafty defense strategy: groveling. My plan was to beg for mercy and ask for the judge's permission to buff his shoes with my hair.

Only there was no judge. They herded us traffic violators into a courtroom with flags and a judge's bench and everything, but instead of an actual human, they had a judge *on videotape*. Really. I could have just stayed home and *rented* the American system of justice.

The video judge welcomed us to Traffic Court and explained our various legal options in such careful detail that by the time he was done none of us had the vaguest idea what they were. Then some clerks started calling us, one by one, to the front of the room. I thought this would be my opportunity to grovel, but before I had a chance, the clerk stamped my piece of paper and told me to go pay the cashier. That was it. Within minutes I was back out on the street, another criminal release with a "slap on the wrist" by our revolving-door justice system.

The first thing I did, back on the Outside, was make an illegal U-turn.

THE DO-IT-YOURSELF DEFICIT-REDUCTION CONTEST

I'm thinking maybe we should do something about this pesky federal budget deficit. Of course this is not our job. We have a political system called "democracy" (from the ancient Greek words "demo," meaning "white men," and "cracy" meaning "wearing blue suits") under which we, The People, do not personally govern the nation because we have to work. So we elect representatives who go to Washington on our behalf and perform the necessary governmental functions that we ourselves would perform if we were there, such as sending out newsletters, accepting large contributions, and becoming involved in a wide range of sex scandals. My favorite part is when the scandal becomes public and the congressperson, in accordance with congressional tradition, attacks the press:

CONGRESSPERSON: Are you media people perfect? Have you never committed an immoral act?

REPORTER: Not involving agricultural products, no.

SECOND REPORTER: At least not *soybeans*.

So there's no need for us to become involved in the

government, unless of course we have a good reason, which is why, about a year ago, I called up the U.S. Treasury Department in an effort to get it to stop making pennies.

Pennies were invented during the Great Depression, a grim era that was filmed entirely in black and white. The nation needed a very small unit of money, because back then—ask anybody who lived through it—the average salary was only four cents per year, and houses cost a dime, and a dollar would buy you a working railroad.

Today, however, nothing costs a penny. Even shoddy, worthless products such as stale gum balls, rest-room condoms, and newspapers cost at least a quarter, the result being that pennies have become nothing but a nuisance, the Mediterranean fruit flies of the coin world. Everybody hates them. Stores deliberately palm them off on you by programming their cash registers so that no matter what you buy, the total comes to something dollars and 61 cents, allowing the clerk to dump upwards of 17 pennies into your hand, knowing that you can't prove that the amount is incorrect because, thanks to the electronic calculator, no normal American outside the third grade remembers how to subtract.

All these pennies end up in your home. In my household alone we have several penny deposits easily the size of brutally persecuted minority group Zsa Zsa Gabor. At risk of suffering fatal hernias we have lugged them from household to household, watching them grow, unable to turn them back into money because the bank won't take them unless you wrap them in those little paper sleeves, a job that we estimate would take us, assuming we did not stop for lunch, until the end of time.

So as a concerned citizen, I called the Treasury Department, where I was eventually connected with an official spokesperson, who told me that the reason the government keeps making pennies is—she really said this—the public *wants* pennies.

"No we don't," I pointed out.

But the spokesperson insisted that yes, we did. She cited several scientific surveys, apparently taken on the Planet Weebo, proving that pennies are highly popular, and assured me that the government plans to keep right on cranking them out.

It is at times like this that we should remember the words of President John F. Kennedy, who, in his stirring inaugural address, said: "Ask not what your country can do for you. Ask whether your country has been inhaling paint-thinner fumes." I mean, look at the federal budget deficit. Everybody in the known universe agrees that the deficit is way too big, so the government's solution is to make it *bigger,* by means of innovative programs such as the savings-and-loan industry bailout. Here we have an industry that managed to lose hundreds of billions of dollars because the people who run it apparently have the financial "know-how" of furniture, so our government's solution is to give them *hundreds of billions more dollars,* which they'll probably rush out and spend on shrewd investments such as worm farms.

So I'm thinking maybe it's time that we, The People, swung into action. Just sitting here scratching my armpit I've already come up with several practical ideas for reducing the deficit:

- Hire men named Vito to kidnap federal pandas Hsing-Hsing and Ling-Ling so the government will stop spending millions each year trying to make them (the pandas) reproduce.
- Require each congressman to sell $17 billion worth of cookies door to door.
- Pass a constitutional amendment requiring a balanced budget.

Well, OK, I admit that last one was "off the deep end." But my point is, our government needs help, which is why I've decided to hold:

A DEFICIT-REDUCTION CONTEST

I want you to think up an idea, write it down on a POSTAL CARD (remember, it has to be short enough

179

that even top federal officials can grasp it) and mail it to me c/o The Miami Herald, Miami, FL 33132. If you win, I'll print your name and suggestion in a column, and armed federal employees with dogs will come to your house at night. Not only that, but if yours is the BEST idea, I'll send you a *CASH PRIZE*. I'm totally serious here. This will be such a massive cash prize that it will be shipped from my house to yours by *truck*. I'm sure it will bring you much happiness, once you get those sleeves on it.

THE SHOCKING SOLUTION TO THE BUDGET DEFICIT

Today we announce the winners in our big Deficit Contest, in which we asked you, the ordinary taxpaying citizens who make up the backbone and pelvic structure of this great nation, to see if you could come up with helpful suggestions for getting rid of this pesky federal budget deficit. As you know, our congresspersons have been unable to work on this because they've been busy passing an Ethics Bill, under which we're going to pay them more money, in exchange for which they're going to try to have some ethics. I think this is a terrific concept, and if it works with Congress, we should also try it with other ethically impaired groups such as the criminally insane.

Speaking of whom, you readers did a heck of a job responding to the Deficit Contest. As I write these words, my office floor is covered with thousands of contest entries, carefully arranged in mounds and in many cases welded together with dog spit supplied by my two research assistants, Earnest and Zippy, who were a major help. But it was you readers who really came through, proving once again that when the American people decide to "get involved" in a problem, it is best not to let them have any sharp implements. Because quite frankly, reading between the lines, I detected a certain amount of hostility in these entries, especially the ones proposing a nuclear strike on the U.S. Capitol.

Some hostility was also directed toward me. In some versions of my original contest column I had proposed, in a lighthearted manner, that we reduce the deficit by "selling unnecessary states such as Oklahoma to the Japanese." This caused a number of Oklahomans to send in letters containing many correctly spelled words and making the central lighthearted point that I am a jerk. They also sent me official literature stating that Oklahoma has enormous quantities of culture in the form of ballet, Oral Roberts, etc., and that the Official State Reptile—I am not making this up—is something called the "Mountain Boomer." So I apologize to Oklahoma, and as a token of my sincerity I'm willing to sell my state, Florida, to the Japanese, assuming nobody objects to the fact that Japan would suddenly become the most heavily armed nation on Earth.

But most of the hostility in the Deficit Contest entries was directed toward our elected federal officials. This is especially true of:

THE CONTEST WINNER

This is Geoffrey Braden of Seattle, Washington, whose idea is that we convert the federal budget deficit to electrical voltage—the bigger the deficit, the higher the voltage—and then run the current through our congresspersons. Geoffrey recommended that we run the current through a specific section of the congressional

182

anatomy that I will not identify here, except to say that besides eliminating the deficit, this proposal would put a real dent in all these sex scandals. Geoffrey therefore wins the big Cash Prize, consisting of all the pennies in my closet, estimated street value $23 million if put into paper sleeves, which will never happen.

Speaking of pennies, about a thousand of you suggested that we eliminate the deficit by sending all our accumulated hateful penny deposits to the government. This is a brilliant idea except for one minor flaw: It's stupid. What it boils down to is giving the government more money, which of course the government would immediately convert into things like accordion subsidies. Which is too bad, because some of you had excellent ideas for increasing government revenue, such as:

- "A $10 million Roman numeral tax on movies. For example, *Rambo IV* would cost Stallone $40 million. I'm not sure whether reducing the number of movie sequels would be a side benefit or the main benefit." (Ed Goodman, Waterbury, Connecticut)
- "Fine people $50,000 for each unnecessary education-related letter attached to the end of their names. For example, 'Robert H. Monotone, B.A., M.B.A., Ph.D.' would be fined $400,000 annually." (Ron DiCesare, Troy, Michigan)
- "The U.S. government should sell its secrets directly to the Russians and cut out the middlemen." (Leslie Price, Hibbing, Minnesota)
- "Rent the Stealth bomber out for proms." (Jimmy Muth, Haverstraw, New York)
- "Sell live film footage of George Bush showering with his dog." (Leslie Gorman, Fort Worth, Texas)
- "Mug Canada." (Kyle Kelly of Dubuque, Iowa, and Mike Orsburn of Gainesville, Texas)

We also got a lot of suggestions that we do not totally 100 percent understand but that we are presenting here as a reminder of the importance of remembering to take our prescription medication:

- "Make deer legal tender." (Jon Hunner, Tesuque, New Mexico)
- "Arbitrarily and capriciously eliminate every other word in government documents." (George Garklavs, Golden, Colorado)
- "Sell manure (all kinds) at North and South poles." (Sharon Rice, Oologah, Oklahoma) (Really)

- "Substitute politicians for road barriers." (Steven Lenoff, Deerfield Beach, Florida)
- "I have a secret plan. Make me president and I'll tell you." (Richard Nixon)
- "Put it in the bunny." (Travis Ranney, Seattle, Washington)

You wacky readers! I love you! Please stay away from my house!

But all kidding aside, the time has come for us to work together on this deficit thing. What can you do? You can write to your congressperson. Tell him you're fed up with government irresponsibility. Tell him you don't want excuses. Tell him you want action.

Tell him these are going to be *very sharp* electrodes.

BUG OFF!

I am sick and tired of our so-called representatives in Washington being influenced by powerful special-interest groups on crucial federal issues. As you have no doubt gathered, I am referring to the current effort to name an Official National Insect.

This effort, which I am not making up, was alertly brought to my attention by Rick Guldan, who's on the staff of U.S. Representative James Hansen of Utah, at least until this column gets published. Rick sent me a letter that was mailed to congresspersons by the Entomological Society of America. (An "entomologist" is defined by Webster's as "a person who studies entomology.") The letter urges Representative Hansen to support House Joint Resolution 411, which would "designate the monarch butterfly as our national insect." The letter gives a number of reasons, including that "the durability of this insect and its travels into the unknown emulate the rugged pioneer spirit and freedom upon which this nation was settled."

The letter is accompanied by a glossy political-campaign-style brochure with color photographs showing the monarch butterfly at work, at play, relaxing with its family, etc. There's also a list entitled "Organizations Supporting the Monarch Butterfly," including the Friends of the Monarchs, the National Pest Control Association, the Southern Maryland Rock and Mineral Club, and the Saginaw County Mosquito Abatement Commission.

Needless to say I am strongly in favor of having an official national insect. If history teaches us one lesson, it is that a nation that has no national insect is a nation that probably also does not celebrate Soybean Awareness Month. I also have no problem with the monarch

butterfly *per se*. ("Per se" is Greek for "unless it lays eggs in my salad.") Butterflies are nice to have around, whereas with a lot of other insects, if they get anywhere near you, your immediate reaction, as an ecologically aware human being, is to whomp them with a hardcover work of fiction at least the size of *Moby Dick*.

But what bothers me is the way the Entomological Society is trying to slide this thing through Congress without considering the views of the average citizen who does not have the clout or social standing to belong to powerful elite "insider" organizations such as the Saginaw County Mosquito Abatement Commission. Before Congress makes a decision of this magnitude, we, the public, should get a chance to vote on the national insect. We might feel that, in these times of world tension, we don't want to be represented by some cute little flitting critter. We might want something that commands respect, especially in light of the fact that the Soviet Union recently selected as its national insect the Chernobyl Glowing Beetle, which grows to a length of 17 feet and can mate in midair with military aircraft.

Fortunately, we Americans have some pretty darned impressive insects ourselves. In South Florida, for example, we have industrial cockroaches that have to be equipped with loud warning beepers so you can get out of their way when they back up. Or we could pick a fierce warlike insect such as the fire ant, although this could create problems during the official White House National Insect Naming Ceremony ("WASHINGTON —In a surprise development yesterday that political observers believe could affect the 1992 election campaign, President Bush was eaten.")

Other strong possible candidates for National Insect include: the gnat, the imported Japanese beetle, the chigger, the praying mantis, Jiminy Cricket, the laughing mantis, the lobster, the dead bugs in your light fixture, the skeet-shooting mantis, and Senator Jesse Helms. I could go on, but my purpose here is not to name all the possibilities; my purpose is to create strife and controversy for no good reason.

And you can help. I recently acquired a highly trained, well-staffed, modern Research Department. Her name is Judi Smith, and she is severely underworked because I never need anything researched other than the question of what is the frozen-yogurt Flavor of the Day at the cafeteria.

So I'm asking you to write your preference for National Insect on a POSTAL CARD. (If you send a letter, the Research Department has been instructed to laugh in the diabolical manner of Jack Nicholson as The Joker and throw it away unopened.) Send your card to: National Insect Survey, c/o Judi Smith, The Miami Herald Tropic Magazine, 1 Herald Plaza, Miami, FL 33132.

Judi will read all the entries and gradually go insane. Then I'll let you know which insect is preferred by you, The People, and we can start putting serious pressure on Congress. If all goes well, this could wind up costing the taxpayers millions of dollars.

In closing, let me stress one thing, because I don't want to get a lot of irate condescending mail from insect experts correcting me on my facts: I am well aware that Senator Helms is, technically, a member of the arachnid family.

INSECT ASIDE

I wish that the critics who claim the average American doesn't care about the issues could see the response we got to our survey about the Official National Insect. We have been flooded with postal cards from all over the United States and several parallel universes. Just a quick glance through these cards is enough to remind you why this great nation, despite all the talk of decline, still leads the world in tranquilizer consumption.

As you may recall, this issue arose when the Entomological Society of America, realizing that troubled times like these call for bold government, began lobbying Congress to name the monarch butterfly as the Official National Insect. Congresspersons received a glossy full-color promotional brochure pointing out that the monarch is attractive, ecological, educational, and courageous, having on several occasions disregarded its own personal safety to pull little Timmy out of the quicksand.

Or maybe that was Lassie. Anyway, the monarch but-

terfly appeared to have a lock on the National Insect-
ship, because the Entomological Society of America is a
powerful outfit. More than one person who has dared
to challenge the society on a piece of insect-related leg-
islation has found his automobile ignition wired to a
hornet's nest in the glove compartment.

Well, you can call me a courageous patriot with cruel
yet handsome eyes if you wish, but I happen to think
that when our Founding Fathers froze their buns at
Valley Forge, they were fighting to create a nation
where the National Insect would be chosen by a fair and
open process, not in some gnat-filled back room. That's

why I asked you, the average citizen with no ax to grind and way too much spare time, to write in and voice your opinion.

All I can say is, it's a good thing that some of you *don't* have axes, if you get my drift. I refer particularly to the person who wrote: "My choice for Official National Incest is mother-son. Thank you for asking."

Many of you voted for the dung beetle, the mosquito, and the leech, all of which were inevitably compared to Congress. I'm sorry but that's a low blow: Our research indicates that no dung beetle has *ever* accepted money from a savings-and-loan operator.

Other insects receiving votes include: the earwig; the gadfly; the tarantula hawk wasp (which kills tarantulas for a living and is already the Official Insect of New Mexico); the maggot; the killer bee (as one reader put it, "We better start sucking up to them while there's still time"); the scorpion; the pissant; the stink bug; the termite; "men"; the tick; the Stealth bomber; the nervous tick; a dead bug named Hector that was actually mailed to us; the screw worm; the fly ("Zip up, America!"); the weevil; the dust mite ("I want a National Insect I can unknowingly inhale"); the worm at the bottom of the tequila bottle; the spittle bug; "Those little moths that get into your cabinets and lay eggs in your Stove Top Stuffing which hatch and cause you to eat the larvae"; the pubic louse; the horned fungus beetle ("because it strongly resembles ex-president Richard Nixon, which makes stomping one into oblivion a special American experience"); Johnny Mantis; the Ford Pinto; Mothra; "any 13-year-old or my ex-husband"; the contact lens borer; the booger, the bug that goes splat on your windshield; and Ted Kennedy.

Without question the most thoughtful vote came

from eight-year-old David Affolter, a student at the Spruce Street School in Seattle, who wrote: "I want the National Insect to be the ladybug, because the ladybug can do about everything a bug should do. It can be a board-game piece."

It's hard to argue with that. But it's also hard to argue with the numbers, and there were 213 votes for the monarch butterfly, versus 87 for the ladybug, 72 for the praying mantis, 65 for the bee, 43 for Senator Jesse Helms, and 37 for the cockroach. Beetles, as a group, got 261 votes, but the beetle vote was badly divided, with no clear "take-charge" beetle emerging.

This is a shame, because one beetle, which received several dozen votes, clearly deserves further consideration. This is the bombardier beetle, which—I am not making this up—has an internal reaction chamber where it mixes chemicals that actually explode, enabling the beetle to shoot a foul-smelling, high-temperature jet of gas out its rear end with a distinct "crack." It reminds me of guys I knew in college. The Time-Life insect book has a series of photographs in which what is described as "a self-assured bombardier beetle" defeats a *frog*. In the first picture, the frog is about to chomp the beetle; in the second, the beetle blasts it; and in the third, the frog is staggering away, gagging, clearly wondering how come it never learned about this in Frog School. I would be darned proud, as an American, to be represented by this insect. An engraving of a bombardier beetle emitting a defiant blast from his butt would look great on a coin.

My point is that, although the monarch butterfly is clearly the frontrunner and has a slick, well-financed campaign, we need to give this National Insect thing a lot more thought. Maybe, as reader James Buzby (his real name) suggests, Congress should appoint a Stop-gap National Insect while we make our final determination.

But whatever happens, I intend to follow this story, even though I may irritate the powerful Entomological Society of America, which for all I know could try to . . . hey, what are these things crawling out of my keyboard? OUCH! HEY!! OUCH!!!

TAX FAX

Income-tax time is here again, and I'm sure that the Number One question on the minds of millions of anxious taxpayers is: Do we have a new Internal Revenue Service commissioner named "Fred"?

I am pleased to report that yes, we do. In fact, if you look on Page 2 of your IRS Form 1040 Instruction Booklet Written by Nuclear Physicists for Nuclear Physicists, you'll find a nice letter from Commissioner Fred, in which he states, on behalf of all the fine men and women and attack dogs down at the IRS: "Let us know if we can do more."

I know I speak for taxpayers everywhere when I say: "NO! Really, Fred! You've done enough!" I am thinking of such helpful IRS innovations as the Wrong Answer Hotline, wherein, if you're having trouble understanding a section of the IRS Secret Tax Code, all you have to do is call the IRS Taxpayer Assistance Program, and in a matter of seconds, thanks to computerized electronics, you are placed on hold for several hours before finally being connected to trained IRS personnel dis-

A little
IRS humor.
(very little)

pensing tax advice that is statistically no more likely to be correct than if you asked Buster the Wonder Horse to indicate the answer by stomping the dirt.

Ha ha! Speaking as a married person filing jointly, let me stress that I am JUST KIDDING here, because I know that the folks at IRS have a terrific sense of humor. Down at headquarters they often pass the time while waiting for their cattle prods to recharge by sending hilarious tax-related jokes to each other in triplicate on IRS Humorous Anecdote Form 1092-376 SNORT.

IRS HUMOR EXAMPLE A: "A lawyer, a doctor, and a priest were marooned on a desert island. So we confiscated their homes."

IRS HUMOR EXAMPLE B: "What do you get when you cross Zsa Zsa Gabor with a kangaroo?" "I don't know, but let's confiscate its home."

What a wacky bunch of personnel! But all kidding aside, it's very important that taxpayers be aware of recent mutations in the tax law. For example, this year everybody connected with the savings-and-loan industry gets a free boat. Also there are strict new regulations concerning how taxpayers should cheat. "If a taxpayer wishes to deduct an imaginary business expense," states the IRS instruction booklet, "then he or she MUST create a pretend financial record by clumsily altering a receipt from an actual transaction such as the rental of the videotape *Big Nostril Mamas.*

When preparing your return, you should be sure to avoid common mistakes. The two most common taxpayer mistakes, states the IRS booklet, are (1) "failure to include a current address,"and (2) "failure to be a large industry that gives humongous contributions to key tax-law-writing congresspersons."

All of us, at one time or another, have been guilty of these mistakes, but I'm sure that this year we'll try to cooperate fully with the IRS, because, as citizens, we feel a strong patriotic duty not to go to jail. Also we know that our government cannot serve us unless it gets hold of our money, which it needs for popular federal programs such as the $421,000 fax machine. I am not making this program up. I found out about it from alert readers Trish Baez and Rick Haan, who faxed me an article by Mark Thompson of Knight-Ridder newspapers concerning a U.S. Air Force contract to buy 173 fax machines from Litton Industries for $73 million, or about $421,000 per machine. Just the paper for this machine costs $100 a roll.

197

If you're wondering how come, when ordinary civilian fax machines can be bought for a few hundred dollars, the Air Force needs one that costs as much as four suburban homes, then you are a bonehead. Clearly, as any taxpayer can tell you, the Air Force needs a special kind of fax machine, a *combat* fax machine. The article quotes an Air Force spokesperson as making the following statement about it:

"You can drag this through the mud, drop it off the end of a pickup truck, run it in a rainstorm, and operate it at 30 below zero."

The spokesperson also said (I am still not making this up): "I was looking at a picture of a squirrel it produced this morning, and if you wanted to sit there long enough you could count the hairs on the squirrel."

1. The Air Force is using a $421,000 fax machine to send pictures of *squirrels?*
2. Are these *enemy* squirrels?
3. Or does the combat fax just start spontaneously generating animal pictures after you drop it off the end of a pickup truck?

The answers are: None of your business. You're a taxpayer, and your business is to send in money, and if the Air Force wants a special combat fax machine, or a whole combat office with combat staplers and combat potted plants and combat Muzak systems capable of playing Barry Manilow at 45 degrees below zero, then it will be your pleasure to pay for them. Because this is America, and we are Americans, and—call me sentimental, but this is how I feel—there is something extremely appealing about the concept of Barry Manilow at 45 degrees below zero.

■■■■ READER ALERT ■■■■

MISTER LANGUAGE PERSON

I like writing Mister Language Person columns, because I always get wonderful mail from irate people who have detected errors in Mister Language Person's grammar. Yes! "Perhaps, Mr. Barry," these letters say, "before you set yourself up as an 'expert,' you should make sure that your OWN grammar is correct." Often the letter-writer rips my column out of the newspaper and sends it back to me with angry corrections written all over it in red ink. You can just imagine how I feel.

ENGLISH,
AS IT WERE

Once again we are pleased to present Mister Language Person, the internationally recognized expert and author of the authoritative *Oxford Cambridge Big Book o' Grammar*.

Q. What is the difference between "criteria" and "criterion"?

A. These often-confused words belong to a family that grammarians call "metronomes," meaning "words that have the same beginning but lay eggs underwater." The simplest way to tell them apart is to remember that "criteria" is used in the following type of sentence: "When choosing a candidate for the United States Congress, the main criteria is, hair." Whereas "Criterion" is a kind of car.

Q. What is the correct way to spell words?

A. English spelling is unusual because our language is a rich verbal tapestry woven together from the tongues of the Greeks, the Latins, the Angles, the Klaxtons, the Celtics, the 76ers, and many other ancient peoples, all of whom had severe drinking problems. Look at the spelling they came up with for "colonel" (which is actually pronounced "lieutenant"); or "hors d'oeuvres" or "Cyndi Lauper." It is no wonder that young people today have so much trouble learning to spell: Study after study shows that young people today have the intelligence of Brillo. This is why it's so important that we old folks teach them the old reliable spelling rule that we learned as children, namely:

> *"I" before "C,"*
> *Or when followed by "T,"*
> *O'er the ramparts we watched,*
> *Not excluding joint taxpayers filing singly.*
> *EXCEPTION: "Suzi's All-Nite E-Z Drive-Thru Donut*
> *Shoppe."*

Q. What the heck are "ramparts," anyway?
A. They are parts of a ram, and they were considered a great delicacy in those days. People used to watch o'er them.

Q. How do you speak French?
A. French is very easy to speak. The secret is, no matter what anybody says to you, you answer, "You're wrong," but you say it with your tongue way back in gargle position and your lips pouted way out like you're sucking grits through a hose, so it sounds like this: "Ur-rrrooonnngggg." Example:

FRENCH PERSON: *Où est la poisson de mon harmonica?* ("How about them Toronto Blue Jays?")
YOU: Urrrrooonnngggg.
FRENCH PERSON: *Quel moron!* ("Good point!")

Q. I know there's a difference in proper usage between "compared with" and "compared to," but I don't care.

201

A. It depends on the context.

Q. Please explain punctuation?

A. It would be "my pleasure." The main punctuation marks are the period, the coma, the colonel, the semi-colonel, the probation mark, the catastrophe, the eclipse, the Happy Face, and the box where the person checks "yes" to receive more information. You should place these marks in your sentences at regular intervals to indicate to your reader that some kind of punctuation is occurring. Consider these examples:

WRONG: O Romeo, Romeo, wherefore art thou Romeo?

RIGHT: O Romeo! Yo! *Romeo!!* Wherethehellfore ART thou? Huh??

ROMEO: I art down here! Throw me the car keys!

Q. Does anybody besides total jerks ever use the phrase "as it were"?

A. No.

Q. What is the correct form of encouraging "chatter" that baseball infielders should yell to the pitcher?

A. They should yell: "Hum babe hum babe hum babe HUM BABE HUM BABE."

Q. May they also yell: "Shoot that ball in there shoot it shoot it SHOOT SHOOT SHOOT WAY TO SHOOT BABE GOOD HOSE ON THAT SHOOTER"?

A. They most certainly may.

Q. What is the difference between "take" and "bring"?

A. "Take" is a transitory verb that is used in statements such as "He up and took off." "Bring" is a consumptive injunction and must be used as follows: "We brung some stewed ramparts to Aunt Vespa but she was already dead so we ate them ourselfs."

Q. What is President Bush's native language?

A. He doesn't have one.

TODAY'S LANGUAGE TIP: A good way to impress people such as your boss is to develop a "Power Vocabulary" by using big words. Consider this example:

YOU: Good morning, Mr. Johnson.

YOUR BOSS: Good morning, Ted.

(Obviously you're not making much of an impression here. Your name isn't even "Ted." Now watch the difference that a couple of Power Vocabulary words can make:)

YOU: Good morning, Mr. Johnson, you hemorrhoidal infrastructure.

YOUR BOSS: What?

YOU GOT A QUESTION FOR MISTER LANGUAGE PERSON? We are not surprised.

IT'S A MAD,
MAD, MAD, MAD
WORLD

There is definitely too much anger in the world today. Pick up almost any newspaper, and the odds are you'll get ink smeared all over your hands. We use a special kind of easy-smear ink, because we know how much it irritates you.

But that's not my point. My point is that if you pick up almost any newspaper, you'll see stories of anger raging out of control, of people actually shooting each other over minor traffic disputes. Can you imagine? Can you imagine feeling so much hostility that just because you're in a traffic jam on a hot day, and you've been stuck for an hour waiting in a long line of cars trying to exit from a busy highway, and along comes one of those line-butting jerks, some guy who's talking on his cellular phone and figures he's *too important* to be waiting in a line with common rest-room bacteria like yourself, so he barges past the entire line and butts in

right in front of you, so you honk your horn, and he shows you his Mister Digit hand puppet, so you haul out a pistol large enough for antiaircraft purposes and LET THE SCUMBALL HAVE IT HAHAHAHAHAHA-HAHA WOULDN'T THAT BE GREAT??

I mean terrible. "Wouldn't that be terrible," is what I mean. And this is why it's so important that we learn to understand what anger is, and how we can cope with it. As you know if you ever studied the famous Greek philosopher Aristotle, he was easily the most boring human being who ever lived. Thousands of college students suffer forehead damage every year from passing out face-forward while attempting to read his books. But it was Aristotle who identified anger as one of the Six Basic Human Emotions, along with Lust, Greed, Envy, Fear of Attorneys, and the Need to Snack.

We know that primitive man felt anger, as is evidenced by the deep kick marks that archeologists have found in prehistoric vending machines. We also see evidence of anger in the animal kingdom. The great white shark, for example, periodically gets furious at the small seaside resort town of Amity and tries to eat all the residents, possibly in an effort to prevent another sequel. And dogs are for some historical reason *extremely* angry at cats. I once watched a dog named Edgar spot a cat roughly a hundred yards away and go tearing after it, faster and faster, gaining ground with each step until he was just inches away, at which point the cat made a very sharp right turn, leaving Edgar to run directly, at Dog Warp Speed, into the side of a house. Fortunately he absorbed the entire impact with his brain, so there was no damage, but this incident teaches us that anger is very self-destructive, and that we must learn to control it.

Let's take the case of the line-butting driver. The trick here is to put things into perspective. Ask yourself: Does it really matter, long-term, if this guy butts in front of you? Is it really more important than serious world problems such as Ethiopia or the Greenhouse Effect? Yes. No question. You don't even know where Ethiopia is. This is why psychologists recommend, when you feel your anger getting out of control, that you practice a simple yoga technique: Imagine that you're in a peaceful, quiet setting such as a meadow, then take a deep breath, then exhale slowly, then gently s-q-u-e-e-z-e that trigger. See how much better you feel? In Advanced Yoga we use grenades.

Aside from traffic, the leading cause of anger is marriage. No matter how much you love somebody, if you spend enough time with that person, you're going to notice his or her flaws. If Romeo had stayed long enough under the balcony staring up worshipfully at Juliet, he'd have become acutely aware of her nasal hairs. So most married couples, even though they love each other very much in theory, tend to view each other in practice as large teeming flaw colonies, the result being that they get on each other's nerves and regularly erupt into vicious emotional shouting matches over issues such as toaster settings.

Professional marriage counselors agree that the most productive and mature way to deal with marital anger is to stomp dramatically from the room. The key here is timing. You want to make your move *before* your opponent does, because the first person to stomp from the room receives valuable Argument Points that can be redeemed for exciting merchandise at the Marital Prize Redemption Center. Of course you have to be on the alert for defensive maneuvers. A couple I know named Buzz and Libby were once having a Force Ten argument in their kitchen, and Buzz attempted to make a dramatic exit stomp, but Libby, a former field-hockey player, stuck her foot out as he went past and tripped him, so he wound up stumbling from the room, trying desperately to look dignified but actually looking like a man auditioning for Clown School. Libby won 5,000 bonus points, good for a handsome set of luggage.

Ultimately, however, anger benefits nobody. If you keep it bottled up inside, it eats away at you, until eventually you turn into a bitter, spiteful, hate-ridden person working in Customer Service. So take my advice: Lighten up. Don't let your anger get the best of you. Don't lose your humanity, or your sense of humor. Don't *ever* try to butt in front of me.

GETTING
M*A*S*H*E*D

Recently my wife, Beth, was ravaged by a sudden, unexpected outbreak of modern medical care.

Well, OK, technically she also had a medical problem,
which I won't go into here except to say that it quickly
faded into dim memory once the treatment began.
Which is exactly the point. As you know if you've ever
been subjected to modern medical care, the whole theory is that if they can make you feel awful enough, you'll
begin to look back on your original ailment with actual
fondness. They take out all your blood and put you in a
tiny room where they expose you repeatedly to daytime
television, and every few hours total strangers come in
to give you Jell-O and stab you with small medical har-
poons and insert tubes at random into your body. Then
they say, "Are you feeling BETTER NOW? Or perhaps
we should give you some MORE MEDICAL CARE HA-
HAHAHAHA." Pretty soon you're on the floor, using
whatever limbs they forgot to disable or remove to
scrabble toward the elevator, your butt sticking into the
air through a hospital garment no larger than a stan-

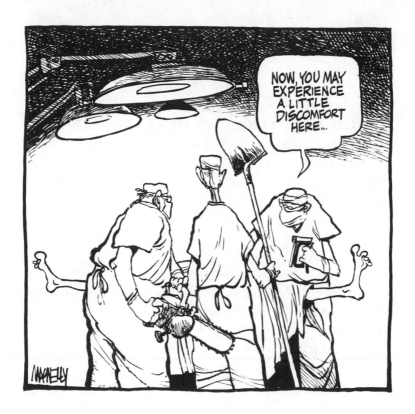

dard Handi-Wipe, your tubes dragging out 15 or 20 feet behind you and spewing a telltale trail of Jell-O that enables the hospital people to track you down and capture you in the parking lot and haul you back to the tiny room and MAYBE RUN A FEW TESTS HAHAHA-HAHAHAHA.

Actually, Beth's doctor, technically known as Doctor Bob, was very nice. In fact everybody at the hospital was nice. But you never really know, with the medical profession. A lot goes on behind closed doors. Just a week before Beth went into the hospital, an alert reader named Pat Wilson in New Delhi, India, sent me an article from the *Hindustan Times* about a doctor at a medical college over there who wanted to determine the "effect of human blood on the stomach when taken orally," so he whipped up a bunch of sandwiches made out of **WARNING:**

DO NOT READ THE REST OF THIS SENTENCE IF YOU ARE OPERATING HEAVY MACHINERY *human bone marrow.* I am not making this up. According to the article, the doctor fed the sandwiches to an unsuspecting colleague, claiming that they contained "a special sauce sent by his sister from America." The doctor was suspended from the college. The colleague is reportedly still off his feed.

This article kept popping into my brain while Doctor Bob and the other skilled professionals were explaining to us in detailed scientific terms how come Beth needed an onslaught of preventive medical care even though she was feeling perfectly fine.

"Do you have any questions?" they kept asking. I had two main ones:

1. "How about we just forget this whole thing?"
2. "You guys definitely eat *regular sandwiches* at this hospital, right?"

But I never found a good time to ask these questions, and so early one morning I drove to the hospital and surrendered Beth, who—this particular detail sticks in my mind, for some reason—was still feeling perfectly fine. They took her away and put masks on and committed acts of medical care on her, and when they brought her back, she was experiencing what the medical community likes to call "discomfort." This is like saying Hiroshima experienced "urban renewal." I have not seen Beth experience so much discomfort since the time she experienced the Joy and Wonder of Natural

Childbirth, during which she left inch-deep grip marks in the steel bedrail.

So I kept lunging out into the corridor and tackling medical professionals around the ankles and dragging them in to look at Beth. "Yes," they'd explain helpfully, while Beth was thrashing around and making sound track noises from *The Exorcist* and, in her occasional moments of rationality, asking to be taken outside and shot, "she is experiencing some discomfort."

Finally I was able, without medical training, to figure out myself what was wrong.

"No wonder she's in pain!" I exclaimed. "Some maniac has put *staples into her!*"

I'm serious. Right into her body. If you, like so many of us, were ever stapled in the hand by Walter Gorski in the fourth grade, you know that even *one* staple is very painful; Beth had enough to supply a bustling legal practice. So you can imagine my shock when I learned that this had done by, of all people, Doctor Bob. Yes! He was *charging us* to staple Beth! What is more, he had installed a *drain.* In my *wife.* I realized right then that Beth had to recover quickly, because God knows what they would do to her next. I might come in one morning and find a kazoo sticking out of her forehead.

Fortunately she got out, and she's going to be fine. Someday she may even feel as good as before they started medically caring for her. So all's well that ends well, and although I've been "poking some fun" here at the medical community, I'm sure you realize that, deep down inside, I have a large inflamed cyst of respect for it. Really. Trust me. Have a sandwich.

P.S. The bill for staples—just the staples—was $63.

TAKING THE
MANLY WAY OUT

Today we're going to explore the mysterious topic of How Guys Think, which has baffled women in general, and the editors of *Cosmopolitan* magazine in particular, for thousands of years.

The big question, of course, is: How come guys never call? After successful dates, I mean. You single women out there know what I'm talking about. You go out with a guy, and you have a great time, and *he* seems to have a great time, and at the end of the evening he says, quote, "Can I call you?" And you, interpreting this to mean "Can I call you?", answer: "Sure!"

The instant you say this, the guy's body start to dematerialize. Within a few seconds you can stick a tire iron right through him and wave it around; in a few more seconds he has vanished entirely, gone into the mysterious Guy Bermuda Triangle, where whole squadrons of your dates have disappeared over the years, never to be heard from again.

Eventually you start to wonder if there's something wrong with you, some kind of emotional hang-up or personality defect that your dates are detecting. Or possibly foot odor. You start having long, searching discussions with your women friends in which you say things like: "He really seemed to like me" and "I didn't feel as though I was putting pressure on him" and "Would you mind, strictly as a friend, smelling my feet?"

This is silly. There's nothing wrong with you. In fact, you should interpret the behavior of your dates as a kind of guy *compliment* to you. Because when the guy asks you if he can call you, what he's really asking you, in Guy Code, is will you marry him. Yes. See, your basic guy is into a straight-ahead, bottom-line kind of thought process that does not work nearly as well with the infi-

nitely subtle complexities of human relationships as it does with calculating how much gravel is needed to cover a given driveway. So here's what the guy is thinking: If he calls you, you'll go out again, and you'll probably have another great time, so you'll probably go out again and have *another* great time, and so on until the only possible *option* will be to get married. This is classic Guy Logic.

So when you say "Sure!" in a bright cheery voice, you may think you're simply indicating a willingness to go out again, but as far as he's concerned you're endorsing a lifetime commitment that he is quite frankly not ready to make after only one date, so he naturally decided he can never see you again. From that day forward, if he spots you on the street, he'll spring in the opposite direction to avoid the grave risk that the two of you might meet, which would mean he'd have to ask you if you wanted to get a cup of coffee, and you might say yes, and pretty soon you'd be enjoying each other's company again, and suddenly a clergyman would appear at your table and YOU'D HAVE TO GET MARRIED AIEEEEEEE.

(You women think this is crazy, right? Whereas you guys out there are nodding your heads.)

So my advice for single women is that if you're on a date with a guy you like, and he asks whether he can call you, you should give him a nonthreatening answer, such as:

"No."

Or: "I guess so, but bear in mind that I'm a nun."

This will make him comfortable about seeing you again, each time gaining the courage to approach you more closely, in the manner of a timid, easily startled woodland creature such as a chipmunk. In a few years, if the two of you really do have common interests and compatible personalities, you may reach the point where he'll be willing to take the Big Step, namely, eating granola directly from your hand.

No matter how close you become, however, remember this rule: Do not pressure the guy to share his most sensitive innermost thoughts and feelings with you. Guys hate this, and I'll tell you why: If you were to probe inside the guy psyche, beneath that macho exterior and the endless droning about things like the 1978 World Series, you would find, deep down inside, a passionate, heartfelt interest in: the 1978 World Series. Yes. The truth is, guys don't *have* any sensitive innermost thoughts and feelings. It's time you women knew! All these years you've been agonizing about how to make the relationship work, wondering how come he never talks to you, worrying about all the anguished emotion he must have bottled up inside, and meanwhile he's fretting about how maybe he needs longer golf spikes. I'm sorry to have to tell you this. Maybe you *should* become a nun.

Anyway, I hope I've cleared up any lingering questions anybody might have regarding guys, as a gender. For some reason I feel compelled to end this with a personal note: Heather Campbell, if you're out there, I just want to say that I had a really nice time taking you to the Junior Prom in 1964, and I was a total jerk for never, not once, mentioning this fact to you personally.

LIFE'S A HITCH,
AND THEN YOU CRY

We're getting into Wedding Season again. This is good for America. We may be falling behind Japan in other areas, such as being able to produce cars or televisions or high school graduates capable of reading rest-room symbols without moving their lips, but we still have the world's largest and most powerful wedding industry.

If you want proof, pick up the February–March issue of either *Bride's* or *Modern Bride* magazine, and right away you'll be struck by the fact that you have sustained a major hernia. Each of these magazines is large enough to have its own climate. *Modern Bride* is over 800 pages long; *Bride's* is over 1,000. Almost every page features a full-color photograph of a radiant young bride, her face beaming with that look of ecstatic happiness that comes from knowing, deep in her heart, that her wedding cost as much as a Stealth bomber, not including gratuities.

"Money can't buy you happiness, so you might as well give your money to us," that is the sentimental motto of the wedding industry. The pages of *Bride's* and *Modern Bride* are crammed with advertisements for silverware, glassware, crystalware, chinaware, ovenware, fondue-ware, Tupperware, underwear, and all the other absolutely mandatory weddingwares that will become Treasured Lifetime Family Heirlooms until they have to be sold to pay the divorce lawyers.

Because let's face it, a lot of marriages just don't work out. Many newlyweds are hurling crystalware within days. Even Donald and Ivana Trump, a couple who seemed to have everything—hair, teeth, most of Manhattan Island—have been having marital problems so tragic that even the most hardened observer is forced to laugh until his gums bleed.

This is why more and more smart engaged couples are avoiding costly future court disputes by means of a legal arrangement called a "prenuptial divorce," under which they agree to get married and divorced simultaneously. This eliminates problems down the road, yet enables the couple to go ahead and have the kind of enormous, ware-intensive wedding that America needs to remain competitive in the world economy.

Weddings also enable us to continue certain cherished traditions, such as the tradition of the bride's family and the groom's family hating each other so much that sometimes, at the reception, the two opposing mothers wind up wrestling in the cake. Of course you can avoid this kind of inter-family tension by means of a new matrimonial wrinkle, the one-family wedding, which was invented by a woman I know named Ginny.

Ginny was in the mood to hold a big wedding, but her only remaining nonmarried child, Edward, wasn't engaged to anybody. So she hit upon the idea of holding a wedding anyway, with the role of the bride played by Tiffany, a life-size bikini-wearing inflatable doll. Tiffany had spent several months floating around the pool,

smiling, and everybody thought she was very nice despite a minor algae problem. Of course there was always the danger that she'd turn out to have a bunch of obnoxious inflatable relatives, but as far as anybody knew she was an orphan.

So we were all very excited about the wedding, when suddenly Edward—you know these headstrong kids—got engaged to Carey, an actual human being. Let me state for the record that Edward made a wonderful choice, but you have to feel bad for Tiffany, who quickly went from the role of Beautiful Bride-To-Be to the role of Deflated Wad in a Closet, which is a tragic waste when you consider that she is more than qualified to be vice president.

But we can't be thinking about tragedies, not with Wedding Season coming. We need to be thinking about the following quotation, which I am not making up, from the Beauty News section of *Bride's* magazine:

"DILEMMA: My brows are too bushy; my bridesmaids' are too sparse. How can we get them in shape by wedding day?"

Unfortunately the solution is too long to reprint here, so you brides-to-be had better pick up a copy of *Bride's,* using a rental forklift, and read the article pronto, because otherwise, as you walk down the aisle on your Very Special Day, you're going to hear people whispering, "What are those things on her forehead? Sea urchins?"

By the way, the rental forklift is the responsibility of the groom.

GETTING PHYSICAL

I started aging rapidly last week. Until then, I had been aging steadily at the rate of about one year per year, with a few exceptions, such as during the party where I drank bourbon from John Cooper's shoe while standing in the shower. When I woke up on the lawn the next morning, I discovered that I had aged nearly a decade.

But after that I felt pretty good until last week, when I went in for my annual physical examination. I get an annual physical exam about once every six years. I'm reluctant to do it more often because of the part where the doctor does A Horrible Thing.

You middle-aged guys know what I mean. You're in the examining room, and the doctor has been behaving in a nonthreatening manner, thumping on your chest, frowning into your ears, etc., and the two of you are having a normal guy conversation about how George Steinbrenner should get, at minimum, the electric chair, and you're almost *enjoying* your physical examination, when, without warning, the doctor reaches into a drawer and pulls out: The Glove.

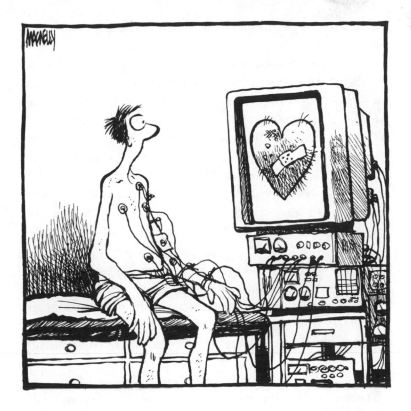

Suddenly you notice that the doctor looks vaguely like Vincent Price, and the room lights are flashing, and the music system, which had been playing "Wonderful World," is now playing the theme from *Jaws*. And now the doctor is holding up his hand, which has grown to the size of a mature eggplant and has sprouted eight or nine extra digits, and he's struggling to pull on The Glove, which has developed a life of its own, snarling and writhing like some kind of evil mutant albino squid. And now the doctor is turning to you, his eyes glowing like beer signs, and he's saying "Turn around hahahaHAHAHAHA" and you're thinking OH NO PLEASE NOOOOOOO.

Once I was getting examined, and when it came time for The Glove the doctor brought in, for training purposes, *another* doctor, who happened to be a member of the extreme opposite sex, and the two of them were back there chatting away about various Points of Interest like a pair of guides on a glass-bottom-boat tour. When it was over, all I wanted was a grocery bag to wear over my head until I could get a new identity through the Federal Witness Protection Program.

But last week I got through The Glove OK. In fact I got through almost everything; the only problem the doctor found—this was NOT during the glove exam—was excessive earwax, which in many cultures is considered a sign of virility. So I was feeling good, ready to schedule my next appointment for late 1996 and sprint for the exit, when the doctor looked at my cardiogram and made that "hmmmm" noise that doctors are taught in medical school so they won't come right out and say "UH-oh!"

"You have an abnormal cardiogram," he said.

He said a lot of stuff after that, but I missed most of it because I was looking around the room for a good place to faint. I do remember the doctor gesturing at an explicit diagram of the human heart and talking about a condition called a "branch bundle blockage" (or maybe he said "bundle branch blockade"), which is caused by the heart valves being connected improperly to the distributor wires. Or something like that. I wasn't really following him. I felt the way I do when the guys at my service station, Sal and Bill, are attempting to explain what's wrong with my car.

"Look at this!" Sal will say, picking up a filth-encrusted object that for all I know is a fragment of Mayan pottery. "Your postulation valve has no comportment!"

224

"No comportment at all!" affirms Bill, genuinely disgusted that such a thing could happen in 20th-Century America.

"And look at this here!" says Sal, thrusting the thing toward me.

"Your branch bundle is blocked!" says Bill.

"You have two weeks to live!" says the doctor.

No, the doctor didn't really say that. He said that an abnormal cardiogram is perfectly normal, and it's probably nothing to worry about, but just in case, he wanted to schedule a test where I run on a treadmill and then they inject atomic radiation into my body and frown at the results.

"Fine!" I said, trying to appear composed, which was difficult because by that point I was sitting on the floor.

So now I'm waiting to take my test, and I'm feeling *old*. I'm experiencing every one of the 147 Major Warning Signs Of Heart Trouble, including Chest Pains, Shortness of Breath, Tendency to Not Notice That the Traffic Light Has Changed, and Fear of Ordering French Fries. Also my heart has taken to beating very loud, especially late at night. Perhaps you have heard it. "STOP BEATING YOUR HEART SO LOUD!" is what I am sure the neighbors are yelling. Fortunately I cannot hear them, on account of my earwax condition.

STRESS FOR SUCCESS

It's 8:30 A.M., and I'm in a small, brightly lit room with a tube in my arm, and a woman I have never met before named Bette is scrubbing my chest with what feels like sandpaper.

"Some people really scream when I do this," Bette is saying.

I'd scream, too, but I'm too busy pretending that there's no tube in my arm.

"There's no tube in my arm," is what I am telling myself in a soothing voice. "There's no tube in my arm. There's a TUBE in my arm. There's a tube IN MY ARM. OMIGOD THERE'S A TUBE STUCK RIGHT INTO MY ARM AND I'M GOING TO. . . "

"I need to lie down," I say.

"You *are* lying down," Bette points out.

I suppose it goes without saying that this is happening in a hospital. Specifically, it's in the Stress Department. That's the real name. When Bette gets on the phone, she says, "This is Bette, in Stress."

I'm here to get what is called a Thallium Stress Test

on my heart. The reason for this, according to my doctor, is that there is probably nothing wrong with my heart. That's what doctors always say: "There's probably nothing wrong . . . but just in case we're going to run a few tests."

"Probably nothing wrong" is the leading cause of health care in America today.

The Stress Test, like most medical procedures, was originally developed by the ex-Nazi researchers at the Institute of Punitive Medicine as a means of maintaining hospital discipline. If you're a hospital patient, and you start to become irritated because the food tastes like Purina Rat Chow and they charge you $2,316.17 every

time you flush the toilet, and you are foolish enough to complain about this, they'll say, "Sounds like we need to *run some tests* on you." And if you have the common sense that God gave gravel you will never open your mouth again. Because the way these tests work is, whatever part of your body they claim they want to look at, they insist upon entering you via some OTHER part. If you have, for example, an ankle problem, they'll say, "What we're going to do is insert this one-inch-diameter exploratory garden hose into your eye socket and run it the length of your body, so you *might experience some discomfort.*"

I won't even TELL you where they insert the hose if you have an eye problem.

So anyway, my doctor—his actual name is Dr. Hamburg, but to avoid a costly lawsuit I will refer to him here as "Dr. Frankfurt"—made the alarming discovery that there was probably nothing wrong with my heart, which is why Bette stuck a tube in my arm and sandpapered my chest and attached wires all over my skin and strapped a large electronic box to me so that I looked like a man being attacked by a crazed mutant home appliance.

I was close to passing out from the stress of all this, but I was thinking to myself, "Well, at least it's almost over, because there's nowhere else on my body for them to attach anything," when in walked Dr. Frankfurt, who ordered me to *run on a treadmill.* With a TUBE in my arm. I bet no medical person has ever even considered doing such a bizarre thing himself.

But Dr. Frankfurt made me do it. While I was running, a small man who had been lurking in the shadows rushed in without warning and put thallium into my arm tube. This made me feel VERY stressful because thallium is basically atomic radiation, and I distinctly remember a horror movie from the 1950s when a man —it might have been James Arness—became radioactive and started glowing like a gambling casino and acting antisocial to the point where he had to be subdued by several branches of the Armed Forces.

The next thing I knew I was in a wheelchair being rushed through the hospital halls with a terrified look on my face and a tube in my arm and radiation in my body, and I was thinking how only an hour earlier I felt fine, and now, thanks to Modern Medicine, people were looking at me in the same pitying way that they'd look at a recently run-over cat. And then I was wheeled into a department called "Nuclear Medicine," which are two words that do NOT go together at all, and they put me on a slab, and all the humans sprinted from the room, probably because of the radiation. Then a medical robot swooped down and examined my body very closely. It did not have a good bedside manner. It would peer at one spot for a while, and then go: "Whir."
"Is that BAD?" I would ask it.
"Whir," it would say.

It turned out that there was nothing wrong with my heart. Just as we had suspected all along. But I'm actually glad that I went through the Thallium Stress Test. For one thing, I know I'm OK. For another thing, I no longer need a bedside lamp. I just read by the glow from my body.

SPORTS NUTS

Today, in our continuing series on How Guys Think, we explore the question: How come guys care so much about sports?

This is a tough one, because caring about sports is, let's face it, silly. I mean, suppose you have a friend who, for no apparent reason, suddenly becomes obsessed with the Amtrak Corporation. He babbles about Amtrak constantly, citing obscure railroad statistics from 1978; he puts Amtrak bumper stickers on his car; and when something bad happens to Amtrak, such as a train crashes and investigators find that the engineer was drinking and wearing a bunny suit, your friend becomes depressed for weeks. You'd think he was crazy, right? "Bob," you'd say to him, as a loving and caring friend, "you're a moron. The Amtrak Corporation has *nothing to do with you.*"

But if Bob is behaving exactly the same deranged way about, say, the Pittsburgh Penguins, it's considered normal guy behavior. He could name his child "Pittsburgh Penguin Johnson" and be considered only mildly eccentric. There is something wrong with this. And before you accuse me of being some kind of sherry-sipping ascot-wearing ballet-attending MacNeil-Lehrer Report–watching wussy, please note that I am a sports guy myself, having had a legendary athletic career consisting of nearly a third of the 1965 season on the track team at Pleasantville High School ("Where The Leaders Of Tomorrow Are Leaving Wads Of Gum On The Auditorium Seats Of Today"). I competed in the long jump, because it seemed to be the only event where afterward you didn't fall down and throw up. I probably would have become an Olympic-caliber long-jumper except that, through one of those "bad breaks" so common in sports, I turned out to have the raw leaping ability of a convenience store. I'd race down the runway and attempt to soar into the air, but instead of going up I'd be seized by powerful gravity rays and yanked *downward* and wind up with just my head sticking out of the dirt, serving as a convenient marker for the other jumpers to take off from.

So, OK, I was not Jim Thorpe, but I care as much about sports as the next guy. If you were to put me in the middle of a room, and in one corner was Albert Einstein, in another corner was Abraham Lincoln, in another corner was Plato, in another corner was William Shakespeare, and in another corner (this room is a pentagon) was a TV set showing a football game between teams that have no connection whatsoever with my life, such as the Green Bay Packers and the Indianapolis Colts, I would ignore the greatest minds in Western thought, gravitate toward the TV, and become far more concerned about the game than I am about my child's education. And *so would the other guys*. I guarantee it. Within minutes Plato would be pounding Lincoln on

the shoulder and shouting in ancient Greek that the receiver did *not* have both feet in bounds.

Obviously, sports connect with something deeply rooted in the male psyche, dating back to prehistoric times, when guys survived by hunting and fighting, and they needed many of the skills exhibited by modern athletes—running, throwing, spitting, renegotiating their contracts, adjusting their private parts on nation-wide television, etc. So that would explain how come guys like to *participate* in sports. But how come they care so much about games played by *other* guys? Does this also date back to prehistoric times? When the hunters were out hurling spears into mastodons, were there also prehistoric guys watching from the hills, drinking pre-historic beer, eating really bad prehistoric hot dogs, and shouting "We're No. 1!" but not understanding what it meant because this was before the development of mathematics?

There must have been, because there is no other ex-planation for such bizarre phenomena as:

- Sports-talk radio, where guys who have never sent get-well cards to their own mothers will express heartfelt, near-suicidal anguish over the hamstring problems of strangers.

- My editor, Gene, who can remember the complete starting lineups for the New York Yankee teams from 1960 through 1964, but who routinely makes telephone calls wherein, after he dials the phone, he forgets who he's calling, so when somebody answers, Gene has to ask (a) who it is, and (b) does this person happen to know the purpose of the call.

- Another guy in my office, John, who appears to be a normal middle-aged husband and father until you realize that he spends most of his waking hours managing a *pretend baseball team*. This is true. He and some other guys have formed a league where they pay actual money to "draft" major-league players, and then they have their pretend teams play a whole pretend season, complete with trades, legalistic memorandums, and heated disputes over the rules. This is crazy, right? If these guys said they were managing herds of pretend caribou, the authorities would be squirting lithium down their throats with turkey basters, right? And yet we all act like it's *perfectly normal*. In fact, eavesdropping from my office, I find myself getting involved in John's discussions. That's how pathetic I am: I'm capable of

233

caring about a pretend sports team that's not even my own pretend sports team.

So I don't know about the rest of you guys, but I'm thinking it's time I got some perspective in my life. First thing after the Super Bowl, I'm going to start paying more attention to the things that should matter to me, like my work, my friends, and above all my family, especially my little boy, Philadelphia Phillies Barry.

THE MALE ANIMAL

Speaking on behalf of all the guys in the world except possibly Phil Donahue, I want to say that I am really ticked off about the results of this recent poll of women. You probably read about it. The Roper Organization asked 3,000 women the following question:

"Do you agree that the average man today is a lazy selfish opinionated egotistical sex-crazed tub of crud who never thinks about anybody but himself and refuses to help with child-rearing or housework and wants to go to bed with practically every woman he meets who is not legally his grandmother and tends to have the same annual output of natural gas as Montana?"

Eighty-seven percent of the women agreed with this. The other 13 percent noted that men also pick their noses at stoplights.

By scientifically analyzing these results, we can conclude that women do not appear to have a high opinion of men. This is unfair. Oh, sure, men in the past have displayed certain unfortunate behavior patterns that tended to produce unhappy relationships, world wars,

etc. But today's man is different. Today's man knows that he's supposed to be a sensitive and caring relationship partner, and he's making radical life-style changes such as sometimes remembering to remove the used tissue wads from his pockets before depositing his pants on the floor to be picked up by the Laundry Fairy.

As so here we men are, making this kind of extreme sacrifice, and WHAM, the Roper Organization hits us with the fact that women still think we're jerks. This really burns my briefs. I mean, I'd like you women to stop and think for a moment about what this world would be like without men. Think of the vast array of cultural and scientific achievements you'd have to do without, including:

1. Football.
2. Professional football.
3. Ear hair.
4. Betting on football.

The list just goes on and on. And let's talk about men's alleged obsession with sex. Do you women think that men are just animals? Do you really think that all they want to do is get you into bed? Wrong! A lot of guys, especially in bars, would be happy to get you into a phone booth! Or right there on the bar! ("Nobody will notice us," the guy will say, being suave. "They're watching 'Wheel of Fortune.'")

But that doesn't mean ALL guys are like that. There are countless examples of guys who think about things beside sex. The guys on the U.S. Supreme Court, for example, think about important constitutional issues, as is shown by this transcript from recent court deliberations.

CHIEF JUSTICE WILLIAM H. REHNQUIST: Whoa! Get a load of the torts on THAT plaintiff!

ASSOCIATE JUSTICE BYRON R. WHITE: (Dies.)

And I am particularly outraged by the charge that guys never help out around the house. I happen to be a guy, and often, when my wife goes away, I assume Total Responsibility for the household, and my wife has such confidence in me that she will often wait for an entire half-hour before she calls:

MY WIFE: Is everything OK?

ME: Fine!

MY WIFE: Is Robert OK?

ME: Robert?

MY WIFE: Our child.

ME: Robert is here?

My wife likes to give me these helpful reminders from time to time because once she went away for several days, and when she got home, she determined that all Robert had eaten the entire time was chocolate Easter bunny heads. But other than that I am very strong in the homemaking department, the kind of guy who, if he gets Cheez Whiz on the sofa, will squirt some Windex on it without even having to be told.

So come on, women. Stop being so harsh on us guys, and start seeing past our macho hairy exteriors, into the sensitive, thoughtful, and—yes—vulnerable individuals that we are deep down inside. And while you're at it, fix us a sandwich.

MALE FIXATIONS

Most guys believe that they're supposed to know how to fix things. This is a responsibility that guys have historically taken upon themselves to compensate for the fact that they never clean the bathroom. A guy can walk into a bathroom containing a colony of commode fungus so advanced that it is registered to vote, but the guy would never dream of cleaning it, because he has to keep himself rested in case a Mechanical Emergency breaks out.

For example, let's say that one day his wife informs him that the commode has started making a loud groaning noise, like it's about to have a baby commode. This is when the guy swings into action. He strides in, removes the tank cover, peers down into the area that contains the mystery commode parts, and then, drawing on tens of thousands of years of guy mechanical understanding, announces that *there is nothing wrong with the commode.*

At least that's how I handle these things. I never actually fix anything. I blame this on tonsillitis. I had tonsillitis in the ninth grade, and I missed some school, and apparently on one of the days I missed, they herded the guys into the auditorium and explained to them about things like carburetors, valves, splines, gaskets, ratchets, grommets, "dado joints," etc. Because some guys actually seem to understand this stuff. One time in college my roommate, Rob, went into his room all alone with a Volvo transmission, opened his toolbox, disassembled the transmission to the point where he appeared to be working on *individual transmission molecules,* then put it all back together, and it *worked.* Whereas I would still be fumbling with the latch on the toolbox.

So I'm intimidated by mechanical guys. When we got

our boat trailer, the salesman told me, one guy to another, that I should "re-pack" the "bearings" every so many miles. He said this as though all guys come out of the womb with this instinctive ability to re-pack a bearing. So I nodded my head knowingly, as if to suggest that, sure, I generally re-pack a couple dozen bearings every morning before breakfast just to keep my testosterone level from raging completely out of control. The truth is that I've never been 100 percent sure what a bearing is. But I wasn't about to admit this, for fear that the salesman would laugh at me and give me a noogie.

The main technique I use for disguising my mechanical tonsillitis is to deny that there's ever anything wrong with anything. We'll be driving somewhere, and my wife, Beth, who does not feel that mechanical problems represent a threat to her manhood, will say, "Do you hear that grinding sound in the engine?" I'll cock my head for a second and make a sincere-looking frowny face, then say no, I don't hear any grinding sound. I'll say this even if I have to shout so Beth can hear me over the grinding sound; even if a hole has appeared in the hood and a large, important-looking engine part is sticking out and waving a sign that says HELP.

"That's the grommet bearing," I'll say. "It's supposed to do that."

Or, at home, Beth will say, "I think there's something wrong with the hall light switch." So I'll stride manfully into the hall, where volley-ball sized sparks are caroming off the bodies of recently electrocuted houseguests, and I'll say, "It seems to be working fine now!"

Actually, I think this goes beyond mechanics. I think guys have a natural tendency to act as though they're in control of the situation even when they're not. I bet that, seconds before the *Titanic* slipped beneath the waves, there was some guy still in his cabin, patiently explaining to his wife that it was *perfectly normal* for all the furniture to be sliding up the walls. And I bet there was a guy on the *Hindenburg* telling his wife that, oh, sure, you're going to get a certain amount of flames in a dirigible. Our federal leadership is basically a group of guys telling us, hey, *no problem* with this budget deficit thing, because what's happening is the fixed-based long-term sliding-scale differential appropriation forecast has this projected revenue growth equalization sprocket, see, which is connected via this Gramm-Rudman grommet oscillation module to . . .

THE WEB BADGE
OF COURAGE

On my 41st birthday, a Sunday in July, I went out to face the spider. It had to happen. There comes a time in a man's life, when a man reaches a certain age (41), and he hears a voice—often this happens when he is lying on the couch reading about Norway in the Travel Section—and this voice says: "Happy Birthday. Do you think you could do something about the spider?" And a man knows, just as surely as he knows the importance of batting left-handed against a right-handed pitcher, that he must heed this voice, because it belongs to his wife, Beth, who, although she is a liberated and independent and tough Woman of Our Times, is deeply respectful of the natural division of responsibilities that has guided the human race for nearly 4 million years, under which it is always the woman who notices when you are running low on toilet paper, and it is always the man who faces the spider.

And so I called softly for my son, Robert. "Robert," I called, and within a matter of seconds he did not appear at my side, because he was in the family room watching

TV commercials for breakfast cereals that are the same color and texture as Pez, but have less nutritional content. So I called louder.

"Robert," I said. "Fetch me the wooden stick that your pirate flag used to be attached to, and the Peter Pan 'creamy'-style peanut butter jar with the holes punched in the lid, for I am going to face the spider."

Upon hearing those words Robert came instantly, and he looked at me with a respect that I have not seen in his eyes for some time now, not since we got the Nintendo. The Nintendo is an electronic video game that is mindless and noncreative and stupid and hateful, and Robert is much better at it than I am. He is 7, and he can consistently rescue the princess, whereas I, a 41-year-old college graduate, cannot even get past the turtles. The worst part is the way Robert says, "Good try, Dad!" in a perfect imitation of the cheerfully condescending voice I used to use on him back when I could beat him at everything. I don't know where kids pick up this kind of behavior.

But there was respect in Robert's eyes as I strode out to face the spider. As well there should have been. Here in South Florida we have a special name for this kind of spider: We call it "a spider the size of Harold C. Crittenden Junior High School," although its technical Latin name is *Bernice*. Bernice had erected a humongous web right outside our front door, an ideal location because in July the South Florida atmosphere consists of 1 part oxygen and 247 parts mosquito, which meant Bernice had plenty to eat. Also on hand in the web was her husband, Bill, who, despite the fact that he was one-sixteenth her size, nevertheless played an important ecological role in the relationship, namely trying not to look like prey.

"I may be small," Bill would say, all day long, in spider language, "but I am certainly not prey! No sir! I am a spider! Yes! Just a regular, NON-prey . . ."

"Shut up," Bernice would say.

"Yes!" Bill would point out. They were a fun couple.

Nevertheless, I approached them cautiously, hoping any noise I made would be drowned out by the roar of the lawn growing. July is in what we South Floridians call the "Rainy Season" because it would depress us too much to come right out and call it the "Giant Armpit Season." When we read the stories about drought-stricken midwestern farmers who can't grow crops in their fields, we are forced to laugh with bitter irony, because down here we can, without trying, grow crops in our *laundry*.

And now I was up to the web. And now, with my son's eyes glued on me, I drew back the pirate-flag stick, and I struck.

"Hey!" said Bernice, in spider. *"HEY!!"*

"Don't hit me!" said Bill. "I'm prey!"

But it was Bernice I had my eye on. If I could poke her into the Peter Pan jar, all would be well. But if she turned and lunged for me, I would have no choice, as a man defending his family, but to drop everything and sprint off down the road, brushing wildly at myself and whimpering.

Fortunately, she went into the jar, and I got the lid on real quick, and for a while we watched her pace around in there and indicate via sweeping arm gestures what she was going to do to us when she got out.

"I'm gonna sting all of your eyeballs," she was saying. "I'm gonna lay 175 billion eggs in your *ears*. I'm gonna . . ."

This was fun, but eventually we decided it was time to get rid of Bernice, following the standard procedure recommended by leading ecologists for the disposal of revenge-crazed spiders, namely: Release them on a drug dealer's lawn. Like many South Floridians, we have our house in a neighborhood that we are pretty sure is occupied by drug dealers, as indicated by subtle clues such as cars coming and going at all hours, bed sheets over the windows, a big sign stating, DRUGS FOR SALE HERE, etc. We decided this would make a fine new home for Bernice, so we drove casually by, and I real quick opened the jar and shook Bernice onto the lawn. She scuttled off angrily straight toward the house. "I'm gonna *fill your nasal passages with web,*" she was saying. "I'm gonna . . ."

But she was no longer our problem. We were already driving off, Robert and I, going shopping for a present for my 41st birthday. We went to Toys "Я" Us.

CONFESSIONS OF
A WEENIE

Recently I've been reading horror novels at bedtime. I'm talking about those paperbacks with names like *The Brainsucker,* full of scenes like this:

"As Marge stepped through the doorway into the darkening mansion, she felt a sense of foreboding, caused, perhaps, by the moaning of the wind, or the creaking of the door, or possibly the Kentucky Fried Chicken bucket full of eyeballs."

Of course if Marge had the intelligence of paint, she'd stop right there. "Wait a minute," she'd say. "I'm getting the hell out of this novel." Then she'd leap off the page, sprint across my bedspread, and run into my son's bedroom to become a character in a safe book like *Horton Hears a Who.*

But Marge, in the hallowed horror-novel-character tradition, barges straight ahead, down gloomy corridors where she has to cut through the foreboding with a machete, despite the obvious fact that something hideous is about to happen, probably involving the forced evacuation of her skull cavity by a demonic being with the underworld Roto-rooter franchise. So I'm flinching as I turn each page, thinking, "What a moron this woman is!" and Marge is thinking: "Well, I may be a moron, but at least I'm not stupid enough to be *reading* this."

And of course Marge is right. I should know better than to read horror books, or watch horror movies, because—this is not easy for a 42-year-old male to admit —*I believe them.* I have always believed them. When I was a child, I was routinely terrified by horror movies, even the comically inept ones where, when Lon Chaney turned into a werewolf, you could actually see the makeup person's hand darting into the picture to attach more fake fur to his face.

When I was 17—this is a true anecdote—I had to explain to my father one Sunday morning that the reason our car was missing was that the night before, I had taken my date to see *Psycho,* and afterward I had explained to her that it made more sense for her to drive me home, because of the strong possibility that otherwise I would be stabbed to death by Anthony Perkins.

For years after I saw *The Exorcist,* I felt this need to be around priests. Friends would say,"What do you want to do tonight?" And I'd say, "Let's take in a Mass!"

I'm still this way, even though I'm a grown-up parent, constantly reassuring my son about his irrational fears, telling him don't be silly, there aren't any vampires in the guest bathroom. Part of my brain—the rational part, the part that took the SAT tests—actually believes this, but a much more powerful part, the Fear Lobe, takes the possibility of bathroom vampires far more seriously than it takes, for example, the U.S. trade deficit.

And so late at night, when I finish my horror novel and take the dogs out into the yard, which is very dark, I am highly alert. My brain's SAT Sector, trying to be

cool, is saying, "Ha ha! This is merely your yard!" But the Fear Lobe is saying: "Oh yes, this is exactly the kind of place that would attract The Brainsucker. For The Brainsucker, this is Walt Disney World."

And so I start sauntering back toward the house, trying to look as casual as possible considering that every few feet I suddenly whirl around to see if anything's behind me. Soon I am sauntering at upwards of 35 miles per hour, and the Fear Lobe is screaming "IT'S COMING!" and even the SAT Sector has soaked its mental armpits and now I'm openly sprinting through the darkness, almost to the house, and WHAT'S THAT NOISE BEHIND ME OH NO PLEASE AAAIIIEEEE

WHUMP I am struck violently in the back by Earnest, our Toyota-sized main dog, who has located a cache of valuable dog poo and shrewdly elected to roll in it, and is now generously attempting to share the experience with me.

Thus the spell of horror is broken, and my SAT Sector reasserts control and has a good laugh at what a silly goose I was, and I walk calmly back inside and close the door, just seconds before the tentacle reaches it.

BLOOD, SWEAT,
AND BEERS

OK, this is it. the last day of the Red Cross blood drive at the *Miami Herald*. Either I am going to do it, or, for the umpteenth consecutive time, I am going to chicken out. All the smart money is on chicken out.

I am a world-class weenie when it comes to letting people stick needles into me. My subconscious mind firmly believes that if God had wanted us to have direct access to our bloodstreams, He would have equipped our skin with small, clearly marked doors. I've felt this way ever since a traumatic experience I had in Mrs. Hart's first-grade class at Wampus Elementary School in the 1950s. There I was, enjoying life and drawing unrecognizable pictures for my mom to put on the refrigerator, when suddenly—you never know when tragedy is going to strike—Mrs. Hart announced in a cheerful voice that somebody named "Dr. Salk" had discovered a "vaccine" for "polio." I had no idea what any of this meant. All I knew was that one minute I was having a happy childhood, and the next minute they were lining us all up in alphabetical order, with You

Know Who in front, marching us to the cafeteria, where we encountered a man—I assumed this was Dr. Salk—holding a needle that appeared to be the size of a harpoon.

"You'll hardly feel it!" said Mrs. Hart, this being the last time I ever trusted a grown-up.

And it got worse. It turned out that you had to get vaccinated several times, plus there was talk that you had to get a "booster shot," which, according to reliable reports circulating around Wampus Elementary, turned your entire arm purple and sometimes made it actually *fall off*. I realize now that Dr. Salk was a great scientist, but at the time I viewed him as a monstrously evil being, scheming in his laboratory, dreaming up newer, more horrible vaccination procedures ("I've GOT it! We'll stick the needle into their EYEBALLS HAHAHAHAHA") and then traveling around the nation, like some kind of reverse vampire, injecting things into innocent victims selected by alphabetical order.

And when we talk about fiendish plots to jab large needles into small children, we certainly have to mention the huge and powerful Tetanus Shot Corporation, which employed undercover agents who were constantly sneaking into my doctor's office, getting hold of my medical file, and altering the date of my last tetanus shot. The result was that whenever I cut myself semi-seriously, which was often, Dr. Cohn would look at my file and say to my mother: "Well, he's due for a tetanus shot."

"But I had one LAST WEEK!" I'd shriek. They never believed me. They were grown-ups, so they believed the stupid file, and sales continued to boom at the Tetanus Shot Corporation.

Of course I am no longer a little boy. I'm a grown-up

now, and I'm aware of the medical benefits of inoculations, blood tests, etc. I'm also aware that the actual physical discomfort caused by these procedures is minor. So I no longer shriek and cry and run away and have to be captured and held down by two or more burly nurses. What I do now is faint. Yes. Even if it's just one of those procedures where they prick your finger just a teensy bit and take barely enough blood for a mosquito hors d'oeuvre.

"I'm going to faint," I always tell them.

"Ha ha!" they always say. "You humor columnists are certainly . . ."

"Thud," I always say.

One time—this is true—I had to sit down in a shopping mall and put my head between my knees because I had walked too close to the ear-piercing booth.

So I have never given blood. But I feel guilty about this, because more than once, people I love have needed blood badly, and somebody, not me, was there to give it. And so now I am forcing myself to walk down the hall to the blood drive room at the *Miami Herald*. And now one of the efficient Red Cross ladies is taking down my medical history.

"Name?" she asks.

"I'm going to faint," I say.

"Ha ha!" she says.

And now I'm sitting down on some kind of medical beach chair, and a Red Cross lady is coming over with . . . with this *bag*. Which I realize she intends to fill with *my blood*. I am wondering if, since this is my first time, I should ask for a smaller bag. Also I am wondering: What if she forgets I'm here? What if she goes out for coffee, and meanwhile my bag is overflowing and dripping down into the Classified Advertising Department? What if . . .

Too late. She has my arm, and she's, oh no, she is, oh nooooooo

Hey! Look up there, in the sky! It's Red Cross ladies! Several of them! They're reaching down! Their arms are thousands of feet long! They're putting cold things on my head!

"It's over," one of them is saying."You did fine."

I'd ask her to marry me, except that (a) I'm already married and (b) I'd be too weak to lift her veil. But other than that I feel great. Elated, even. I have a Band-Aid on my arm, a Beige Badge of Courage. And somewhere out there is a bag of my blood, ready to help a sick or injured person become his or her same old self again, except that he or she might develop a sudden, unexplained fondness for beer.

Not that you asked, but the Red Cross number for information about giving blood is 1-800-GIVE LIFE.

AN OFFER THEY
CAN'T REFUSE

Recently I received an exciting offer in the mail from my credit-card company. Usually their offers involve merchandise that no actual human would ever need.

"Dear Mr. Dave Barry," they say. "How many times have you asked yourself: 'Why can't I cook shish ke-bab AND enjoy recorded music?' Well, Mr. Dave Barry, because you are a valued customer who has consistently demonstrated, by paying us three million percent interest, that you have the financial astuteness of a lint ball, we are making available to you a Special Opportunity to purchase this deluxe combination gas barbecue grill and CD player."

But this recent offer was even better. This was an offer to sell me *my own credit rating*. Yes. One of the great benefits of living in America is that, regardless of your race or religion or hygiene habits, you are entitled to have a credit rating maintained by large corporations with powerful computers that know *everything about you*. For example, let's say that this morning you deposited your paycheck at the bank, made a phone call, wrote a

check for your electric bill, and charged some gasoline on your credit card. By this afternoon, thanks to high-speed laser fiber-optic data transmission, the computers will know *every sexual fantasy you had* while you were doing these things. And don't think they keep it to themselves, either. They are as human as the next person. They go to computer parties, they have a few too many diskettes, and the next thing you know they're revealing your intimate secrets at the rate of four billion per second.

That's why I was so excited about this offer from my credit-card company to sell me the TRW CREDEN-TIALS service. TRW is a large company that collects credit information about people and sells it. According to the TRW CREDENTIALS offer, if I give them $20 a year, they'll let me see my information.

The offer states: "Financial experts recommend that you carefully review your credit report *twice a year* to check its information and make certain that it is accurate."

In other words—correct me if I am wrong here—they're telling me that I should give them $20 a year so I can look at the information ABOUT ME that they collected WITHOUT MY PERMISSION and have been selling for years to GOD ALONE KNOWS WHO so I can see if it's INCORRECT.

Which it very well could be. Because even with computers, things sometimes go wrong. I know you find this hard to believe, inasmuch as we live in such a competent nation, a nation capable of producing technological wonders such as the Hubble Orbiting Space Telescope, the only orbiting telescope in the universe equipped with dark glasses and a cane. But sometimes mistakes do get made, and they could affect your credit.

For example, just recently we got a phone call at home, at night, from a woman from a collection agency. She said we'd be in big trouble if we didn't turn over four cable-TV boxes, which she said we had failed to return to the cable company when we moved a year ago. I explained that, (1) it was only two boxes, and (2) we had made three appointments with the cable company to come get them, but nobody ever showed up, and (3) we would love to get rid of them, and (4) maybe SHE could get the cable company to come get them. The woman said, basically, that it was too late for that, because this matter had been turned over to *a collection agency,* which is apparently several levels above the U.S.

Supreme Court, and we had better hand over four cable boxes or this would go on our Permanent Credit Record.

So I called up the cable company, and joined the millions of Americans on hold, waiting to talk to one of the nation's estimated four cable-company service representatives, two of whom are on break. Future generations, when they look at formal family portraits from this era, will say, "There's Aunt Martha, who was a teacher, and the man holding the phone receiver to his ear is Uncle Bob, who was on hold to the cable company."

Finally, miraculously, I got through, and even more miraculously, they came out and got our boxes. And I was feeling very good about America until the collection-agency woman called again, at night, to inform me that we'd be in big trouble if we didn't turn over the boxes. All four of them.

So I don't know what our credit record says. I wouldn't be surprised if it holds us largely to blame for the savings-and-loan scandal. So I'm definitely interested in the TRW CREDENTIALS offer.

However, I don't like to do business with an outfit unless I know something about it. So I've decided to develop a file on TRW. I'd certainly appreciate anything you can contribute. But I don't want any wild speculative unfounded rumors, such as:

- TRW is the world's largest distributor of hard-core pornography.
- TRW has destroyed two-thirds of the Earth's ozone layer.
- TRW is a satanic vampire cult headed by the love child of Jim Bakker and Leona Helmsley.

———

There is no need to run the risk that absurd statements such as these might get into print. In fact, it would probably be a wise idea for TRW to examine my file, from time to time, just to make sure *nothing inaccurate* appeared in there.

I'm sure we can work something out.

THE ROLL OF
THE HUMORIST

If you're looking for a sport that offers both of the Surgeon General's Two Recommended Key Elements of Athletic Activity, namely (1) rental shoes and (2) beer, then you definitely want to take up bowling.

I love to bowl. I even belong to a bowling team, the Pin Worms. How good are we? I don't wish to brag, but we happen to be ranked, in the World Bowling Association standings, under the heading "Severely Impaired." Modern science has been baffled in its efforts to predict what will happen to a given ball that has been released by a Pin Worm. The Strategic Air Command routinely tracks our bowling balls on radar in case one of them threatens a major population center and has to be destroyed with missiles.

But the thing is, we have fun. That's what I like about bowling: You can have fun even if you stink, unlike in, say, tennis. Every decade or so I attempt to play tennis, and it always consists of 37 seconds of actually hitting the ball, and two hours of yelling "Where did the ball go?" "Over that condominium!" etc. Whereas with bowling, once you let go of the ball, it's no longer your legal responsibility. They have these wonderful machines that find it for you and send it right back. Some of these machines can also keep score for you. In the Bowling Alley of Tomorrow, there will even be machines that wear rental shoes and throw the ball for you. Your sole function will be to drink beer.

Besides convenience, bowling offers drama. I recently witnessed an extremely dramatic shot by a young person named Madeline, age 3, who is cute as a button but much smaller. We were in the 10th frame, and Madeline had frankly not had a good game in the sense of knocking down any of the pins or even getting the ball

to go all the way to the end of the lane without stopping. So on her last turn, she got up there, and her daddy put the ball down in front of her, and she pushed it with both hands. Nothing appeared to happen, but if you examined the ball with sensitive scientific instruments, you could determine that it was actually rolling. We all watched it anxiously. Time passed. The ball kept rolling. Neighboring bowlers stopped to watch. The ball kept rolling. Spectators started drifting in off the street. TV news crews arrived. A half dozen Communist governments fell. Still Madeline's ball kept rolling. Finally, incredibly, it reached the pins and, in the world's first live slow-motion replay, *knocked them all down*. Of course by then Madeline had children of her own, but it was still very exciting.

For real bowling excitement, however, you can't beat Ponch, the bowling dog. I'm not making Ponch up; he holds the rank of German shepherd in the Miami Police Department, and he bowls in charity tournaments. He uses a special ramp built by his partner, K-9 Officer Bill Martin. Bill puts the ball on the ramp, then Ponch jumps up and knocks the ball down the ramp with his teeth. It looks very painful, but Ponch loves it. He loves it so much that as soon as the ball starts rolling, he wants to get it back, so he starts sprinting down the lane after it, barking, his feet flailing wildly around, cartoon-style, on the slick wood (this is a violation of the rules, but nobody is brave enough to tell Ponch).

When Ponch is about halfway down the lane, he suddenly sees his ball disappear into the machinery, so he whirls around and flails his way back to the ball-return tunnel, where he sticks his head *down into the hole*, barking furiously, knowing that his ball is in there somewhere, demanding that it be returned *immediately,* and then suddenly WHAM there it is, hitting Ponch directly in the face at approximately 40 miles per hour, and *he could not be happier.* He is overjoyed to see his ball again, because that means Officer Bill's going to put it on the ramp and Ponch can hit it with his teeth again! Hurrah!

Not only is Ponch a lot of fun to watch, but he's also very naive about scoring, so you can cheat. "Sorry, Ponch," you can say, "I scored 5,490 in that last game, so you owe me a million dollars." He'll just wag his tail. Money means nothing to him. But touch his ball and he'll rip out your throat.

FULL-BORE
BOOK TOUR

I didn't lose my luggage until Day 12 of the Book Promotion Tour From Hell. By then I was glad to get rid of it. I'd been dragging it to every North American city large enough to have roads, appearing on thousands of radio talk shows, all named "Speaking About Talking," for the purpose of pretending to be enthusiastic about my book, although after about the fifth day I usually just staggered into the radio station, put my head down on the host's lap, and went to sleep. Most hosts are accustomed to interviewing unconscious book-tour victims, so they'd just plunge ahead. "Our guest today on 'Speaking About Talking,'" they'd say, "smells like the bottom of a homeless person's shopping bag."

This was true. The reason was that, no matter how many days I'm on the road, I insist on taking only one small carry-on suitcase so as to prevent my luggage from falling into the hands of the Baggage People, who would pounce upon it like those grief-stricken Iranian mourners who nearly reduced the late Mr. Ayatollah Khomeini to Corpse McNuggets. So my garments and

toiletry articles spend their days compressed into an extremely dense carry-on wad in which they are able to freely exchange grime, mayonnaise stains, B.O. vapors, etc., the result being that after several days my "clean" shirts look like giant community handkerchiefs and my Tartar Control toothpaste tastes like sock dirt. Eventually my luggage undergoes a process known to physicists and frequent fliers as "suitcase fusion," wherein the contents all unite into one writhing, festering, pulsating blob of laundry that, when I get to the hotel room, climbs angrily out of the suitcase by itself and crawls over to the TV to watch in-room pornographic movies. This worries me, because the movie goes on my computerized hotel bill, and I'm afraid that when I check out, the clerk will say, in a loud and perky voice: "Mr. Barry, we certainly hope you enjoyed your stay here, especially your private in-room viewing of *Return to Planet Nipple*."

Actually I don't have time to watch movies, because I have to forage for food. The split-second schedule of the Book Promotion Tour From Hell calls for me to arrive at the hotel five minutes after room service closes, so I usually enjoy a hearty and nourishing meal from the "mini-bar," which is a little box provided as a service to hotel guests by the American Cholesterol Growers Association, featuring foodlike items that are perfect for the busy traveler who figures he's going to die soon anyway, such as Honey-Roasted Pork Parts.

After dinner it's time to crawl into bed, turn out the lights, and listen to the Subtle But Annoying Air-Conditioning Rattle, which is required by law to be in all hotel rooms as a safety precaution against the danger that a guest might carelessly fall asleep. You notice that the bellperson never tells you about this. The bellperson gives you a lengthy orientation speech full of information that you have known since childhood, such as that you operate the TV by turning it on, but he never says, "Incidentally, the only way to stop the annoying rattle is to jam a pair of Jockey shorts into that air register up there." No, part of the fun of hotel life is that you get to solve this puzzle for yourself, which I usually do at 1:30 A.M., just in time for the start of the Sudden Violent Outburst of Hallway Laughter Tournament, in which teams of large hearing-impaired men gather directly outside my door to inhale nitrous oxide and see who can laugh loud enough to dislodge my shorts from the air register. In less time than it took to form the

Hawaiian Islands the night has flown by and it's 5:42 A.M., time for the Housekeeping Person, secure in the knowledge that I cannot pack a gun in my carry-on luggage, to knock on my door, just above the sign that says PLEASE DO NOT DISTURB in 127 languages, and inform me helpfully that she'll come back later. But I usually get up anyway, because the sooner I check out, the sooner I can appear on a radio talk show and get some sleep.

Sometimes I also go on TV, which is how I lost my luggage. What happened was, a TV crew was following me around, doing a story about a Typical Day on a book tour. They put a wireless microphone on me so they could record me making typical remarks, such as: "Is this recording me in the bathroom?" And: "I'm wearing a wireless microphone." I made this last typical remark to a concerned security person after I set off the alarm at the Minneapolis–St. Paul airport. So he started poking around under my shirt, bravely risking Death by Armpit Fumes, and while this was going on some other unfortunate air traveler mistakenly walked off with my suitcase. I hate to think what happened to this person. My guess is that at some point he foolishly opened my suitcase and a tentacle of my laundry came snaking out and dragged him back inside.

The airline people eventually gave me back my suitcase, but now I'm afraid to open it, because this person is probably still in there, being genetically combined with my Prell shampoo. So if you're missing a friend or loved one who was last seen in the Minneapolis–St. Paul airport, I've got him, and I'll be glad to return him when I come to your town, which will be any day now on the Book Tour From Hell. You'll smell me coming.

COFFEE?
TEA?
WEASEL SPIT?

So I was getting on a plane in Seattle, and I was feeling a touch nervous because that very morning a plane was forced to make an emergency landing at that very airport after a window blew out at 14,000 feet and a passenger almost got sucked out of the plane headfirst. This is the kind of thing that the flight attendants never mention during the Preflight Safety Demonstration, although maybe they should. I bet they could put on a very impressive demonstration using an industrial vacuum cleaner and a Barbie doll, and we passengers would NEVER take our seat belts off, even when the plane landed. We'd walk out into the terminal with our seats still strapped to our backs.

Anyway, the good news is that the passenger in Seattle was wearing his seat belt, and the other passengers were able to pull him back inside, and he's expected to make a complete recovery except for no longer having a head. This will definitely limit his ability to enjoy future in-flight meals ("Would you like a dense omelet-like substance, sir? Just nod your stump.").

Ha ha! I am just joshing of course. The man retained all his major body parts. But just the same I don't like to hear this type of story, because I usually take a window seat, because I want to know if a wing falls off. The pilot would never mention this. It is a violation of Federal Aviation Administration regulations for the pilot to ever tell you anything except that you are experiencing "a little turbulence." You frequent fliers know what I'm talking about. You're flying along at 500 miles an hour, 7 miles up, and suddenly there's an enormous shuddering WHUMP. Obviously the plane has struck something at least the size of a Winnebago motor home—in fact sometimes you can actually see Winnebago parts flashing past your window—but the pilot, trying to sound bored, announces that you have experienced "a little turbulence." Meanwhile you just know that up in the cockpit they're hastily deploying their Emergency Inflatable Religious Shrine.

Here's what bothers me. You know how, during the Preflight Safety Demonstration, they tell you that in the event of an emergency, oxygen masks will pop out of the ceiling? My question is: *Who wants oxygen?* If I'm going to be in an emergency seven miles up, I want *nitrous oxide,* followed immediately by Emergency Intravenous Beverage Cart Service, so that I and my fellow passengers can be as relaxed as possible. ("Wow! Those are some beautiful engine flames!")

Anyway, nothing terrible happened on my flight, which was unfortunate, because there was a high school marching band on board. My advice to airline passengers is: Always request a non-marching-band flight. Oh, I'm sure that these were wonderful teenage kids on an individual basis, but when you get 60 of them together in a confined area, they reach Critical Adolescent Mass, with huge waves of runaway hormones sloshing up and down the aisle, knocking over the flight attendants and causing the older passengers to experience sudden puberty symptoms (the pilot's voice went up several octaves when he tried to say "turbulence").

Mealtime was the worst. The entree was Beef Stroganoff Airline-Style, a hearty dish featuring chunks of yellowish meatlike byproducts that apparently have been pre-chewed for your convenience by weasels. I was desperately hungry, so I was actually going to attempt to eat mine, when one of the male band members seated near me, in the age-old adolescent tradition of Impress-

ing Girls Through Grossness, launched into an anecdote about an earlier in-flight meal:

". . . so she was eating chocolate all day, right? And she gets on the plane and they serve her the meal, right? And she looks at it, and she goes, like, RALPH all over her tray, and it's like BROWN and it's getting ALL OVER her TRAY and onto the FLOOR, so she like stands up and she goes RALPH all over the people in front of her and it's like running down their HAIR and . . ."

This anecdote didn't bother the band girls at all.

"Ewwwwww," they said, chewing happily. Whereas I lost my appetite altogether. I just sat there, a frequent flier looking at his Vaguely Beeflike Stroganoff and wondering how come airline windows never suck people out then you really need them to.

I'M DAVE.
FLY ME.

I'm going to start my own airline. Hey, why not? This is America, right? *Anybody* can have an airline. They even let Donald Trump have one, which he immediately renamed after himself, as is his usual classy practice despite the fact that "Trump" sounds like the noise emitted by livestock with gastric disorders ("Stand back, Earl! That cow's starting to Trump!").

Well if he can do it, I can do it. My airline will be called : "Air Dave." All the planes in the Air Dave fleet will utilize state-of-the-art U.S. Defense Department technology, thus rendering them—this is the key selling point—invisible to radar. That's right: I'm talking about a *stealth airline.*

Think about it. If you're a frequent flier, you know that the big problem with commercial aviation today is that the planes can be easily detected by Air Traffic Control, which is run by severely overstressed people sitting in gloomy rooms drinking coffee from Styrofoam cups and staring at little radar-screen dots, each one representing several hundred carefree people

drinking Bloody Marys at 35,000 feet. Naturally the air-traffic controllers become resentful, which is why they routinely order your Boston-to-Pittsburgh flight to circle Mexico City until the captain reports that the entire passenger sector is experiencing Barf Bag Overload.

They won't be able to do that stuff to Air Dave. They won't even be aware that an Air Dave flight is in the vicinity until it screams past the control tower at Mach 2, clearly displaying its laser-guided air-to-tower missiles, and requests permission to land *immediately*.

Air Dave planes will not park at a gate. Air Dave planes will taxi directly to the rental-car counter.

The official Air Dave spokesperson will be Sean Penn.

There will be no mutant in-flight "food" served on Air Dave. At mealtime, the pilot will simply land—on an interstate, if necessary—and take everybody to a decent restaurant.

Air Dave will do everything possible to live up to its motto: "Hey, You Only Go Around Once." There will be no in-flight movies. There will be *live bands*. Every flight will feature a complimentary Petting Zoo Cart. Air Dave will also boast the aviation industry's finest in-flight pranks. For example, just after takeoff the door to the cockpit might "accidentally" swing open, revealing to the passengers that the sole occupant up there, cheerfully sniffing the altimeter, is a Labrador retriever named "Boomer."

All Air Dave planes will have skywriting capability.

Air Dave pilots will be chosen strictly on the basis of how entertaining their names sound over the public-address system, as in "First Officer LaGrange Weevil" or (ideally) "Captain Deltoid P. Hamsterlicker." Pilots will be encouraged to share their thoughts and feelings with the passengers via regular announcements such as: "What the heck does THIS thing do?" and "Uh-oh!"

In the event of an emergency, a ceiling panel will open up over each seat and out will pop: Tony Perkins.

I've given a lot of thought to the flight attendants. My original idea was to use mimes, who would go around *pretending* to serve beverages, etc. But then I got to thinking about an opinion voiced a few months back by Al Neuharth, the brain cell behind *USA Today* ("The Nation's Weather Map"). You may remember this: Mr. Neuharth wrote a column in which he was highly critical of today's flight attendants, whom he described as "aging women" and "flighty young men." And quite frankly I think he has a point, which is why all the flight attendants on Air Dave will be hired on the basis of looking as much as possible like the ultimate human physical specimen: Al Neuharth. Assuming we can find anybody that short.

The Preflight Safety Lecture on Air Dave will consist of five minutes of intensive harmonica instruction. Passengers will also be notified that under Federal Aviation Administration regulations, anyone requesting a "light" beer must be ejected over Utah.

Air Dave pilots will have standing orders to moon the Concorde.

So that's the Air Dave Master Plan. On behalf of Captain Hamsterlicker and the entire crew of Neuharths, let me say that it's been a real pleasure having you read the column today. And remember: Under the Air Dave Frequent Flier program, if you log just 25,000 miles, *we'll let you off the plane.*

━━━ READER ALERT ━━━

DAVE BARRY
FOR PRESIDENT

In this historic column I became the first humor columnist that I know of to openly declare his candidacy for the presidency in 1992. The public responded with a massive outpouring of support conservatively estimated at seven or eight letters, only a few of which directly threatened my life. A couple of people actually sent money in denominations as high as one dollar; as a token of my gratitude, I plan to nominate these people to the U.S. Supreme Court. I'll nominate them even if the court has no vacancies. That's the kind of "people president" I plan to be. One of my mottoes is: "Dave Barry: He'll Award A High Federal Office To Virtually Any Dirtbag Who Gives Him Money." Another one is: "Dave Barry: He'll Keep Dan Quayle." This is to ensure my personal security.

WE WILL
BARRY YOU

I know what's bothering you, as a concerned American. What's bothering you is that it's 1991 already, and nobody is running for president. It's eerie. At this time four years ago Iowa was already infested with presidential timbers such as Bruce Babbitt and Pierre S. "Pete" du Pont IV Esquire, Inc. The average Iowa farmer could not take a step without bumping into several leading presidential contenders demonstrating their concern for agriculture by lifting small pigs. And yet today, four years later, nobody is actively campaigning out there. (Not that the pigs are complaining.)

Of course George Bush has been busy, what with the Persian Gulf, the economy, bonefishing, etc. And there is speculation about Mario Cuomo running. But there has always been speculation about Mario Cuomo running. A large portion of the Rosetta stone is devoted to ancient Egyptian speculation about Mario Cuomo running. You also hear talk about Sen. Albert Gore, but the U.S. Constitution clearly states in Article III, Section 4,

279

Row 8, Seat 5, that the president cannot be somebody named "Albert."

"Arnold, maybe," states the Constitution. "But not Albert."

Another possible candidate, Sen. Bill Bradley, possesses the one quality that thoughtful American voters value above all in a leader: height. Unfortunately, Senator Bradley also has, with all due respect, the charisma of gravel. Hospitals routinely use tapes of his speeches to sedate patients for surgery. Rep. "Dick" Gephardt has no eyebrows and is, in the words of a recent *New York Times* editorial, "probably an alien being."

Clearly, the nation has a Leadership Vacuum. Well,

where I come from, we have a saying: "If you're not going to grab the bull by the horns while the iron is in the fire, then get off the pot." (There are a lot of chemicals in the water where I come from.) And that is why I am announcing today that I am running for President of the United States.

(Wild sustained applause.)

Thank you. But before I accept your support and your large cash contributions, I want you to know where I stand on the issues. Basically, as I see it, there are two major issues facing this nation: Domestic and Foreign. Following are my positions on these issues as of 9:30 this morning.

DOMESTIC AFFAIRS: I would eliminate all giant federal departments—Transportation, Commerce, Interior, Exterior, etc.—and replace them with a single entity, called the Department of Louise. This would consist of a woman named Louise, selected on the basis of being a regular taxpaying individual with children and occasional car trouble and zero experience in government. The Department of Louise would have total veto power over everything. Before government officials could spend any money, they'd have to explain the reason to Louise and get her approval.

"Louise," they'd say, "We want to take several billion dollars away from the taxpayers and build a giant contraption in Texas so we can cause tiny invisible particles to whiz around and smash into each other and break into even tinier particles."

And Louise would say: "No."

Or the officials would say: "Louise, we want to use a half million taxpayer dollars to restore the childhood home of Lawrence Welk."

And Louise would say: "No."

Or the officials would say: "Louise, we'd like to give the Syrians a couple million dollars to reward them for going almost a week without harboring a terrorist."

And Louise would say: "No."

Or the officials might say: "Louise, we want to . . ."

And Louise would say: "No."

All of these decisions would have to be made before 5:30 P.M., because Louise would be very strict about picking up her kids at day care.

FOREIGN AFFAIRS: These would be handled via another new entity called The Department of A Couple of Guys Named Victor. The idea here would be to prevent situations such as the Panama invasion, where we send in the army to get Manuel Noriega, and a whole lot of innocent people get hurt, but NOT Manuel Noriega. He gets lawyers and fax machines and a Fair Trial that will probably not take place during the current century.

The Department of A Couple of Guys Named Victor would not handle things this way. I'd just tell them, "Victors, I have this feeling that something unfortunate might happen to Manuel Noriega, you know what I mean?" And, mysteriously, something would.

Or, instead of sending hundreds of thousands of our people to fight hundreds of thousands of Iraqis all because of one scuzzball, I'd say: "Victors, it would not depress me to hear that Saddam Hussein had some kind of unfortunately fatal accident in the shower."

I realize there will be critics of this program. "What if he doesn't take showers?" they will say. But these are mere technical details. The important thing is that I have a platform, and next week I'm going to Iowa—really—as the first declared candidate, and if you want to get on the bandwagon, now is the time, because there is a lot of important work to be done, such as selecting the band for the Victory Party. Right now I am leaning toward Little Richard.

Also, I need to locate a small pig.

AFTERWORD

(NOTE TO PEOPLE WHO HAVE ACTUALLY
READ THIS BOOK:
**Please disregard the following section. It's intended
purely as a sales device to entice people at bookstores
who decide whether or not to buy a book by flipping
directly to the end to see how it comes out.)**

Lance looked at Laura, and there was lust in his eyes,
because he knew, from the 173 sex scenes that took
place in this action-packed novel, that she was a woman
of major sexual appetites, not to mention hooters the
size of Lincoln, Nebraska.

"Oh, Lance," she said. "We have been through so
much in this steamy, action-packed novel, which is a real
bargain at the suggested retail hardcover price of only
$15.95, higher in Canada."

"You're not kidding," remarked Lance. "It would be
a steal even without the section that explains in simple,
easy-to-understand terms how anybody who has the

284

brain-wave activity of a carrot can make up to $50,000 a month in his or her spare time without doing anything remotely productive!"

"Not to mention the chapter explaining the Amazing Surgeon General's Diet Plan that enables a person to lose as many as 17 pounds per hour without hunger or even conscious awareness!" laughed Laura.

"Buy this book right now!" they chorused. "Mrs. L. Puttee of Big Stoat, Ark., bought this book, and the next day she won four billion dollars in the lottery! Myron Fennel of Syracuse, N.Y., failed to buy this book, and the next day his head was sliced off by a helicopter rotor and landed on the roof of a Holiday Inn four miles distant!"

Your eyes are getting heavy. You are getting sleepy, very, very sleepy. You are walking up to the bookstore clerk. You are taking out your wallet. We take all major credit cards. Thank you.